Ruth Wolff

EMPRESS
OF CHINA

357 W 20th St., NY NY 10011
212 627-1055

Empress of China

First printing: July 1986

ISBN: 0-88145-039-1

Design by Marie Donovan
Cover art designed by Design Team One, Inc., with illustration by Dave Miller, AIR Studio, Inc., for The Cincinnati Playhouse in the Park.
Set in Aster by L&F Technical Composition, Lakeland, FL
Printed and bound by Cushing-Malloy, Inc., Ann Arbor, MI

For
Martin and Evan
Whose Love
Makes Everything Possible

CONTENTS

Empress of China premiered on April 25, 1984 at The Pan Asian Repertory Theatre in New York. Tisa Chang directed the following cast:

SHEN TAI .... Mel Gionson
LI LIEN-YING .... Tom Matsusaka
TZU-HSI............................. Tina Chen
KUANG-HSU .... Lester J.N. Mau
KANG YU-WEI .... Ernest Abuba
LUNG-YU .... Carol A. Honda
THE PEARL CONCUBINE .... Mary Lee
JUNG LU .... Alvin Lum

Bob Phillips was the Set Designer; Victor En Yu Tan, the Light Designer; Eiko Yamaguchi, the Costume Designer; Yung Yung Tsuai, the Movement Director. Robert Pace composed the music, and James D'Asaro was the Stage Manager.

Empress of China ran at The Cincinnati Playhouse in the Park from 2-28 October 1984. Robert Kalfin directed the following cast:

SHEN TAI .... Jonathan Fuller
LI LIEN-YING .... Joe Palmieri
TZU-HSI .... Ching Valdes
KUANG-HSU .... Keenan Shimizu
KANG YU-WEI .... Ron Nakahara
LUNG-YU .... Vincenetta Gunn
THE PEARL CONCUBINE .... Freda Foh Shen
JUNG LU .... Ray Dooley
PLAYERS .... Joseph Fuqua, Paula Godsey, Jeffrey Hasler, Ellen Lochhead, Mark Mocahbee, Michael Pollard, Juanita Scheyett, Anne Shapland, Robert Stormont, Mary Kay Wildenhain
MUSICIANS .... Richard Arnest, Mark Dayton, Doug Smith

Michael Sharp designed the scenery; Andrew B. Marlay, the costumes; Edward Effron, the lighting; and Dania Krupska, the choreography. Mel Marvin composed the music. Laurie F. Stone was the Production Stage Manager, and Kimberly Osgood the Assistant Stage Manager.

About the Author

America's preeminant author of biographical plays and films about women, Ruth Wolff has written tour de force roles that have been interpreted by such luminaries as Liv Ullmann, Glenda Jackson, and Lilli Palmer. She has been represented on the stages of Europe in highly acclaimed performances by Gemma Jones (England), Anne Wil-Blankers (Holland), and Edmonda Aldini (Italy).

In half a dozen biographical plays, Wolff has given dramatic presence to such fascinating figures as Eleanor of Aquitaine, Christina of Sweden, George Sand and Frederic Chopin, Sarah Bernhardt, and Mary and Percy Bysshe Shelley, in addition to the Dowager Empress Tzu-hsi.

Although these people lived in the past, Wolff's theatricality is blazingly modern. Her themes are sharply contemporary—from the nature of woman, to the consequences of sexual and intellectual freedom, to the use and misuse of power in all its forms. Wolff's vision is wide-ranging, spanning many centuries and many civilizations. Throughout, her intent is to show what is eternal in human nature. Her canvas is vast in space and time, but her themes are always insightfully relevant to the here and now.

Wolff's play *The Abdication*, which is about Queen Christina's abdication of the throne of Sweden and her love for Cardinal Azzolino after she converted to Catholicism and came to live in Rome, was given its world premiere by the Bristol Old Vic. Its highly successful Italian production played Rome and toured all of Italy. Ms. Wolff wrote of the Italian premiere in her *New York Times Magazine* article, "We Open in Florence". In another major foreign production, at De Haagse Comedie in the Hague, Anne Wil-Blankers won Holland's most important acting award, the Theo d'Or, for her starring performance as Christina of Sweden. *The Abdication*, frequently produced in the United States, is published in *The New Women's Theatre* (Random House).

A screenwriter as well as playwright, Ruth Wolff wrote the screenplay for the Warner Bros. film of *The Abdication*, which starred Liv Ullmann and Peter Finch.

Another Wolff play, *Sarah in America*, which is about Sarah Bernhardt's American tours, was produced by the Kennedy Center. It starred Lilli Palmer, and was directed by Sir Robert Helpmann. The play is a tour de force for one actress (with the silent part of a maid). *Sarah in America* takes the indomitable Bernhardt from age 36 to 72, covering four of her nine American tours. With Lilli Palmer starring, *Sarah in America* was seen nationally on PBS on *Kennedy Center Tonight*.

Ms. Wolff interpreted other events in Bernhardt's early career and marriage in her screenplay for the film *The Incredible Sarah*, which starred Glenda Jackson.

George and Frederic, Wolff's play about the nine-year relationship between Sand and Chopin, had its world premiere at the University of Utah, where Ms. Wolff also lectured on "Writing the Biographical Play". The play also was presented in a staged reading at the Williamstown Theatre Festival starring Blythe Danner and Austin Pendleton.

Empress of China was given its world premiere in New York by the Pan Asian Repertory Theatre, directed by Tisa Chang and starring Tina Chen. The same year saw the Cincinnati Playhouse production of the play directed by Robert Kalfin and starring Ching Valdes.

Ms. Wolff's adaptation of *The Golem* was presented off-Broadway. The O'Neill Theatre Center produced her plays *Folly Cove* and *Still Life with Apples*. The New Theatre Workshop produced her two-character play, *Arabic Two*. Her article, "The Aesthetics of Violence", appeared in *Ms. Magazine*. She received a Rockefeller Foundation Playwrighting Fellowship to Wesleyan University, a Kennedy Center Bicentennial Commission, and is a fellow of the MacDowell Colony.

A native of Massachusetts who has lived in Paris and now lives in New York, Ms. Wolff was educated at Smith College and Yale University. Her newest play, *The Perfect Marriage*, is about Mary and Percy Bysshe Shelley in the afterworld.

POWER AND POWERLESSNESS

"A concubine who rose to power . . ." This description of Tzu-hsi, Empress of China, is popular because of its sexual overtones. But the truth is Tzu-hsi was probably far less interested in sex than she was in power. Sexuality was only a route to that goal.

Tzu-hsi was born in 1835. At sixteen, by the simple act of becoming one of the Emperor's concubines, she moved herself closer to the throne than any man born to her rank and station. At this early phase, being a woman—and the mother of the Emperor's only son—was a distinct advantage. Beyond this, her major advantages were her courage and her brains.

There are some people born with personalities so definite, so clear and incisive, that others follow them no matter where they are leading. Tzu-hsi was one of these. She had innate personal magnetism. Charisma. She knew what she wanted and she dared destroy anything that stood in her way.

Nietzsche said, "The will to power is the will to life." The desire for power was certainly what drove Tzu-hsi, and we tend to associate that drive with villainy. Was she a villainess? Are all the tales of tortures and poisonings and murders true?

Rather than painting her as an unalloyed villain, I have chosen to dwell on the motivation Tzu-hsi shares with us all: the desire to have control over one's own life, to exert a life-force stronger than the forces exerted upon one. It is necessary to wade neck-deep into existence to find out just how strong and constant those contrary forces really are.

Power is the ability to act to produce change. It is measured by one's ability to triumph over circumstance. One becomes heroic to the measure of how large a battle one takes on in molding one's own destiny and the destinies of others. Tzu-hsi took on the greatest responsibility there was—the guiding of her country. And she took it on unafraid.

The irony is that when she was most in power she felt most powerless. She reached the throne, but even from this lofty place was unable to mold events to her will. She had to reach absolute power before she could feel its absolute emptiness. Tested to the limit, she responded by lashing out with deathly force, by allying herself with violence, the violence that eventually became her undoing.

Believing China to be the greatest power on earth, Tzu-hsi misjudged the strength of the forces against her. The ancient civilization was beset by internal problems: government corruption and rebelliousness of the people in the provinces, as a result of famine and widespread poverty. Natural disasters—floods—made it seem as if the heavens were against China. Foreign powers—not only the Western powers, but Russia and Japan as well—invaded and occupied areas of the land. For nearly a century the British, desiring China's tea and silk, had been forcing the Chinese to trade these for opium grown in the British colony of India. When the Chinese fought back—on their own territory— they lost. Blindly hating the forces of *Westernization*, Tzu-hsi stood against the forces of *modernization*, not seeing until it was too late that the two were different. Her reactionary traditionalist policies kept her looking backward because when she looked forward, all she saw was the hated influence of the West.

Tzu-hsi shared with the lowliest peasant, with everybody, with us, the pathetic desire to somehow make life come out right. That she couldn't manage it, that she underestimated the magnitude of the forces against her, doesn't make her less. It makes her human.

Some say Tzu-hsi brought about the death of a civilization. Others say it was because of her that that civilization survived a few more years. One can imagine the complacent smile of Buddha as Tzu-hsi beat her fists against the forces of destiny, of progress, of Westernization, and made so little effect. She misread the direction of the tides of history, but she seemed the only one courageous and capable enough to steer the ship.

Grand in her ambitions, and just as grand in her delusions, Tzu-hsi is something of a modern Macbeth. Being a tyrant, she naturally chose as her favorite deity Kuan-yin, the Goddess of Mercy. The Dowager Empress was infinite in her contradictions. She was unmatched in her will. She was thoroughly convinced of her own importance. It took nothing less than international war and internal revolution to convince this tiny woman that she could not make her own life and the life of her country what she wanted them to be. Yet she tried. And in that attempt lies her nobility.

RUTH WOLFF

CHARACTERS

(In order of appearance)

SHEN TAI, The Actor
LI LIEN-YING, Chief Eunuch
TZU-HSI The Empress Dowager
KUANG-HSU, The Emperor
KANG YU-WEI, The Tutor
LUNG-YU, The Empress, Wife of Kuang-Hsu
THE PEARL CONCUBINE
JUNG LU, The General
Male and Female Servants

(*Note*: The number of Servants is at the discretion of the director. They may be used silently within scenes, as indicated. They also may be used to change scenery between scenes.)

Setting

A cube of space set in a black or white void.

A unit set made of platforms and vertical elements which, with slight alteration or by use of projections, may be transformed to make the same space accommodate different places and scenes.

For each scene, the specific place is suggested by the appearance of one or two significant objects—a screen, a throne, a gate, an instrument of torture, etc. All should be accomplished with great simplicity.

The vertically hung circular Drum of Remonstrance is visible throughout the play.

The production should be sharply modern, with any richness of detail and color occurring only in the props and costumes.

Time and Place

The action takes place in the Forbidden City, Peking, China, between 1898 and 1900.

The scenes unfold in various locations in the Forbidden City: The Empty Chamber, The Hall of Supreme Harmony, The Palace of Tranquil Old Age, The Garden, The Ocean Terrace, The Imperial Viewing Platform, and The Gate of Spiritual Valor.

ACT ONE

(At Rise: THE EMPTY CHAMBER. Prison. In the center of the barren chamber a young man, SHEN TAI, *naked above the waist, is suspended, spread-eagle, in chains. Beneath his chin is the sharp silver blade of an axe, so positioned that, should he fall asleep, should he move from a head-erect position in any way, he will decapitate himself.)*

*(*SHEN TAI *is a Chinese in his late twenties, a muscular descendant of simple peasant ancestry, now desperately weary, parched and starving from days of being suspended in air.)*

(His head begins to nod. He warns himself hoarsely:)

SHEN TAI: Stay awake! . . . Stay awake, you ass! . . .

I don't think you realize what a magnificent position you are in. . . . You don't have to stand. You don't have to sit. You don't have to worry about eating. Or drinking.

What an amazing privilege! To be prisoner within the walls of the Forbidden City! Very few commoners ever enter here. Of course, even fewer leave.

(Fearfully) They say the Empress Dowager's favorite punishment is the death of a thousand cuts. The executioner skins the victim, slice by slice, keeping him alive to witness his own demise as long as possible.

I wonder if that will happen to me? . . . It's certainly worth staying alive to find out!

(He thinks he hears a noise.) What's that? . . . Who's there? *(There is no reply. He calls out:)* I have faith in the mercy of the Empress Dowager!

(Silence. He calls out again:) The Empress Dowager is exalted above all women! She is the Motherly, Auspicious, Orthodox, Heaven-Blessed, Brightly Manifest, Calm, Sedate, Perfect, Illustrious, Exalted—

(*Suddenly, from somewhere outside the chamber, a high male voice announces imperiously:*)

LI'S VOICE: Do not look upon the Empress!

(*The* Empress?! SHEN TAI *is astonished, frightened, curious. He hardly has time to compose himself when* LI LIEN-YING, *the Chief Eunuch, a crafty old man with hairless face and soft lips, enters.*)

LI: Do not look upon the Empress!

SHEN TAI: The Empress? Here?

LI: Do not speak!

(SHEN TAI *closes his mouth.*)

LI: You are a creature of less than no importance. You are excrement! A turd!

SHEN TAI: Gracious thanks.

LI: Silence! Why she considers soiling her eyes by gazing upon you, I do not know!

(*From behind the screen comes the deep hard voice of an older woman, echoing majestically:*)

EMPRESS'S VOICE: I adore filth!

LI: Do not hear!

SHEN TAI: How can I not—?

EMPRESS'S VOICE: Remove his ears!

SHEN TAI: I heard nothing! Nothing!

LI: Do you know why you are here?

SHEN TAI: No, Excellency.

LI: I am Li Lien-Ying, Chief Eunuch. Not 'Excellency'.

SHEN TAI: Yes, Eunuch.

LI: 'Honorable Sir'!

SHEN TAI: Yes, Honorable Sir—or Madame.

LI: What—?

SHEN TAI: I said nothing.

LI: Is it true you have insulted the Empress?

SHEN TAI: No, it is not true.

LI: Is it true you have dared personify her in performances in public squares?

SHEN TAI: No insult was meant—

LI: Is it true you have assumed her dress, her voice—?

EMPRESS'S VOICE: Why do you think you can portray me? Have you ever seen me?

LI: Do not answer!

EMPRESS'S VOICE: By what right do you usurp my life, my breath?! Do you think you can equal me?!

(*Suddenly, the Dowager Empress* TZU-HSI *appears. The effect is overwhelming. She is a woman in her sixties, wiry, strong, with steel-cold eyes, black-dyed hair, and foot-long sharpened shafts for fingernails. Her silken gown is elaborately embroidered.*)

(*Overwhelmed by her presence,* SHEN TAI *stares at her, stunned, for a moment, then regains his senses and looks firmly away.*)

SHEN TAI: I see nothing! I hear nothing!

LI: Fall to your knees in the presence of the Empress Dowager, Tzu-hsi!

(TZU-HSI—*pronounced "Soo-Shee"—approaches the helplessly spreadeagled* SHEN TAI, *and says imperiously:*)

TZU-HSI: I release him from the obligation of falling on his knees.

LI: Thank her for her mercy.

SHEN TAI: Thank you—

LI: Do not speak to her!

Tzu-hsi: "I release him from the obligation of falling on his knees." (Shen Tai: Jonathan Fuller; Tzu-hsi: Ching Valdes, from the Cincinnati production. Photo copyright 1984 by Sandy Underwood.)

SHEN TAI: (*Confused and upset*) I thank the Empress!

(TZU-HSI *walks slowly around him, examining every inch of him like a specimen, then says:*)

TZU-HSI: I will allow him one question.

LI: You have one question.

(*Silence.* SHEN TAI *considers his question. Then, at last, he asks:*)

SHEN TAI: Will I live?

(TZU-HSI *breaks out in a sudden laugh.*)

TZU-HSI: He is superb! The direct mind of a peasant! (*To* SHEN TAI:) You will live if I say you will live. And I will decide after I see you perform.

SHEN TAI: I am only a poor travelling player—

TZU-HSI: Good. Poverty sharpens artistic perception.

SHEN TAI: I did not train at the academy. I learned my craft in the streets. I was an orphan. Half-starved. If you knew how poor—

LI: Do not sully the Empress's ears with tales of misfortune in the country!

TZU-HSI: Discuss it with my nephew, the Emperor. These things do not concern me. I am retired. (*To* LI:) Remove the axe.

(*Manservants enter, remove the axe, and exit.*)

LI: Do you have a name?

SHEN TAI: Shen Tai.

TZU-HSI: Soft. Appropriate for a man who plays women.

LI: Perhaps he served his clientele in other ways—

SHEN TAI: Offstage I am a man! (*Aside*) Unlike you.

(*Before* LI *can respond,* TZU-HSI *says:*)

TZU-HSI: I will see your performance, Shen Tai.

SHEN TAI: I have no costumes—

TZU-HSI: I have costumes. The remains of an actor who displeased me.

(*She points toward a large trunk.* SHEN TAI *opens it. It is full of costumes and props.*)

I used to enjoy sex, food and theatre—in that order. Now I enjoy theatre, food—and food.

(*She claps her hands and calls out:*)

Bring my food!

(*Servants bring in trays containing dish after dish of a sumptuous banquet.* SHEN TAI *looks on hungrily.* TZU-HSI *deliberately taunts him as she chooses her favorite food.*)

I love theatre most—although I do not know why the art is usurped by those who have no training for it, no rights to it. But then, there are many rights which now are being usurped in the country—and not to its good.

(SHEN TAI *is trying on a robe.*)

Why am I being kept waiting?!

(*Hurriedly, he fastens it.* TZU-HSI *suddenly feels despondent.*)

Li, I think this entertainment will not amuse me.

LI: My dear Empress, there is no amusement quite as amusing as being on the throne.

TZU-HSI: True. Off of it, everything I do seems merely like filling time. . . . Why am I being kept waiting?

(SHEN TAI *puts on a ridiculous headdress. The effect is insulting.*)

I am being pilloried!

(*She rises in fury.*)

SHEN TAI: Empress, do not condemn me for the ineptitude of my acting! I am only a poor—

TZU-HSI: In the name of Buddha, begin!

(SHEN TAI *begins. He takes a pose as a young and innocent maiden. He begins in a high falsetto. His gestures are wildly exaggerated. The effect is absurd.*)

SHEN TAI: I am a young and innocent maiden, the daughter of a poor but honest Manchu official. Already, at sixteen, I am known for my radiant, shining, unbelievable. unsurpassable, incredible beauty. (*He looks at her, hoping his flattery will impress her.*)

TZU-HSI: I want to see it exactly as you play it!

SHEN TAI: My beauty is so renowned that I am summoned with other maidens to the Great Within on the Emperor's birthday. Because of my radiant, shining, unbelievable, unsurpassable, incredible beauty—

TZU-HSI: (*Aside*) It's lucky I have a good digestion!

SHEN TAI: Because of my great beauty, I am chosen to be concubine by the Emperor himself!

(*Hungrily, he eyes her plate as she enjoys her dinner.*)

TZU-HSI: Starvation is good for you. It will help you keep your girlish figure. Continue.

SHEN TAI: Bidding farewell to my beloved family, I go to live forever within the walls of the Forbidden City. Here I am known as the Orchid Concubine. The Emperor loves me above all others. And in a while, as a reward for my modesty, charm, humility, and quiet virtue, heaven smiles upon me. I am permitted to present the Emperor with— his only son.

(*He bows, awaiting her response. She rises, eyes aflame.*)

TZU-HSI: (*With fury*) Is that how you portray me?

SHEN TAI: Yes, Empress, as a woman of grace and beauty—

TZU-HSI: You lie! Do you think I believe your audience comes to see that?!

SHEN TAI: It is how I see you—as the great benevolent Regent of China for four decades! As a woman of supreme wisdom and kindness. As—

TZU-HSI: Enough! Do not insult me by trivializing my life! Do you think I could have ruled for five minutes as that sweet, puking idiot you portray? . . . About my father, you are right. He was poor. And honest? Of course he was honest. He was dead! (*She comes toward him.*) I shall show you how I was chosen to be concubine.

(*She takes his place; he begins to sit in hers.*)

LI: Do not sit in the presence of the Empress!

(SHEN TAI *rises precipitously.* TZU-HSI *says commandingly:*)

TZU-HSI: This is the *true* story of my life. Pay attention! . . . I am sixteen. On the Emperor's birthday, I am summoned with other maidens to the Great Within. Here he will choose his bride and concubines. It is the only opportunity I will ever have in this world to make a life. I *must* be chosen! But first, I must be certified a virgin.

My lover, the warrior Manchu Bannerman Jung Lu, has given me a precious sapphire. When I am lying on the table of the woman who examines maidenheads, she finds it. I am passed through.

Although another is chosen as wife, the Emperor chooses me himself as concubine. He chooses me because, when all others look modestly down, I look up. He likes what he sees.

When months go by and still I have not been chosen to come to his chamber, I bribe the Chief Eunuch to be sure the Emperor will walk down a path where he can hear me singing. That very night, he writes my name on his slate. At darkness I am carried to his bed, naked, wrapped only in a yellow quilt.

There follows a night like no other night he has known. My screams of fear, my modest protestations, the exquisite shudder of my first ecstasy! . . . First love can be extraordinary—if one has experience!

By morning, I am his favorite and inseparable concubine. . . . But hardly because of my modesty and virtue! And as for my making a son for my impotent, dissolute husband by heaven smiling! You must be mad!

SHEN TAI: Empress—

TZU-HSI: Silence! I will not be insulted by your view of me! There is no virtue in virtue! There is no value in innocence! I prefer guile! I will not allow you to continue this sweet and treasonable portrayal!

SHEN TAI: I will portray the Empress in whatever way she wishes—

TZU-HSI: The perfect mentality for a slave!

SHEN TAI: I am at your command—

TZU-HSI: I command you to stand erect and be of use to me! I command you to portray me correctly—or die! And while you are perfecting your portrayal, I command you to give acting lessons to my nephew, the Emperor. His walk is not authoritative. His voice is higher than mine!

SHEN TAI: I will give him Emperor lessons.

TZU-HSI: And while you are in his court, you will hear everything, see everything. After that, you will tell me everything. The Kuang-Hsu Emperor has no abilities at all —except at times the ability to keep his own counsel. You must report to me *everything*.

SHEN TAI: Then I will live?

TZU-HSI: Your life is of no importance to me. Nor is your death. (*She sees him looking at the food.*) Would you care to eat the dishes I have not eaten?

SHEN TAI: Yes, Empress! You are generous, Empress!

(*Hungrily, he dives into several dishes that she has not touched. Suddenly, he begins to vomit.*)

TZU-HSI: You do not like the taste of maggots?

(*He looks at her.*)
You're fortunate you chose that dish. (*She points to a second dish.*) This one is seasoned with little springs which uncoil inside your intestines. (*She points to a third dish.*) This one is laced with ground cat hairs—which have an interesting effect upon the stomach walls. (*She returns to the one he ate.*) All you have is a few worms happily crawling through your inner passages.

(*At the thought,* SHEN TAI *once more begins to vomit..*)

(TZU-HSI *turns and begins to exit, followed by the Eunuch. Behind her she hears the sound of* SHEN TAI *vomiting.*)

I like that sound. It is a good sound. It is the sound of a future friend.

(*She goes out.*)

(*Lights change.*)

(THE HALL OF SUPREME HARMONY. Court of the Emperor Kuang-Hsu.)

(In the room is displayed the Emperor's exquisite clock collection. It is a sunny morning.)

(KUANG-HSU, *the Emperor, a pleasant but effeminate-looking man in his middle twenties, is deep in studies with his* TUTOR, KANG YU-WEI, *an intense man in his mid-thirties, an activist and scholar.)*

TUTOR: It is more splendid to be living at this time than at any other since the creation of the planet, my Emperor! This is the time when the future meets the past. Ideas which have been dreams for centuries can now become reality.

KUANG-HSU: But, my tutor, how can *I* make some contribution?

TUTOR: By being the one to bring China into the modern world.

KUANG-HSU: It is a great responsibility.

TUTOR: You can achieve it. You can be the means of abolishing suffering and bringing the country into the age of equality and peace.

KUANG-HSU: Tell me once more what life will be like when we achieve this . . .

TUTOR: In the One World, people will live high in the air in great palaces with air cooling and heating from electricity. Some people will live in flying vessels. Others will live on great ships—with gardens inside.

KUANG-HSU: And you really think all this can happen in my lifetime?

TUTOR: All this and more. There will be machines which harness the energy of the sun so people will be spared all back-breaking labor. There will be new methods for preserving health and spiritual well-being. This Age of Disorder will be replaced by the Age of Ease and Happiness for all.

Tutor: "It is more splendid to be living at this time than at any other since the creation of the planet, my Emperor." (Tutor: Ron Nakahara; Kuang-Hsu: Keenan Shimizu, from the Cincinnati production. Photo copyright 1984 by Sandy Underwood.)

KUANG-HSU: It must be we Chinese who invent these things!

TUTOR: That I cannot promise.

KUANG-HSU: But we invented silk and paper and gunpowder—

TUTOR: True, Emperor. But today the train, the telegraph, and the steam engine are more to the point.

KUANG-HSU: Why are these not *our* discoveries?

TUTOR: It is the Western mind—which constantly looks forward—

KUANG-HSU: —while ours constantly looks back.

TUTOR: I think we are going to have to change direction.

KUANG-HSU: How can we ever catch up?

TUTOR: What they have, we can borrow. It isn't a matter of getting there first, it's a matter of getting there at all. The British, in the past ten years, have so mechanized their industry that they are able to manufacture in minutes what it takes us—

(*At this moment* KUANG-HSU'S WIFE, LUNG-YU, *enters, carrying brushes and paper. She is a homely creature several years older than he.*)

WIFE: Books in English again. Aunt will not like it.

KUANG-HSU: She will only know, dear wife, if you tell her.

WIFE: If you do not want to make her angry, do not do things she does not like! (*She sits, practicing calligraphy.*)

KUANG-HSU: Stop the lesson. A cloud has entered the room.

(*Like a radiant presence, the* PEARL CONCUBINE *enters. She is as intellgent as she is beautiful.*)

KUANG-HSU: Never mind. Here is the sun.

(KUANG-HSU *and the* PEARL *smile at each other.*)

PEARL: A gift—from the British legation.

(*A servant enters carrying a magnificent golden clock with mechanical birds on top.* KUANG-HSU *is enthralled, but his* WIFE *shakes her head disapprovingly. He looks away.*)

TUTOR: You are permitted to like it. Your aunt is not in the room!

PEARL: Oh, look! It tells the weather, too! And the seasons! And the year. The Western year. (*She giggles.*) It's only one thousand eight hundred and ninety-eight!

KUANG-HSU: I shall change it to the year of my dynasty. As I do, I shall study its workings.

(*The servant exits.*)

WIFE: Aunt says you have all the makings of a clockmaker.

KUANG-HSU: And *you* have all the makings of an aunt!

PEARL: Come, my love—

KUANG-HSU: How fortunate for me that I found the Pearl Concubine. Otherwise I would be disappointed in the race of women.

(TZU-HSI *enters unannounced.*)

TZU-HSI: Which is nothing to what the race of women is in you!

(*All humble themselves in deep kow-tow, including* KUANG-HSU. *In forceful aside, the* TUTOR *says to him:*)

TUTOR: You do not bow to her! You are the Emperor!

(KUANG-HSU *rises. The others rise.*)

TZU-HSI: Look at this lovesick boy on whose shoulders has fallen the Mandate of Heaven! Look at him—ruler of the world! In love! How can you expect to control others if you can't control your own passions? Love clouds the mind, drains the will, and deadens the senses. Be detached!

WIFE: He is detached—from me.

TZU-HSI: Is that why you haven't borne him a child?

WIFE: I am practicing calligraphy as you told me.

(TZU-HSI *inspects the* WIFE'S *work.*)

TZU-HSI: This looks like the work of silkworms. (*She spies the clock.*) Who is this one from?

KUANG-HSU: The British.

TZU-HSI: What do they want in return? Peking?

KUANG-HSU: To talk.

TZU-HSI: We do not have dialogues with inferiors.

KUANG-HSU: We could discuss our mutual problems—

TZU-HSI: We have no mutual problems. Our problem is them! They force us to sell them our tea and to buy their opium. They insist we all become good Protestants and Catholics. They want our goods, our lands, our souls. All we want is their absence. They petition. We say no. That is all.

PEARL: It is not all, Empress, when, since the war, we owe them so much indemnity—

Tzu-hsi: Listen to her! Why don't you appoint her Ambassador Extraordinary? She could seduce the entire allied army and they might leave us in peace!

Pearl: Is it not possible that the West might show us how to—

Tzu-hsi: Silence! I will acknowledge your existence when you produce a son.

Kuang-Hsu: That isn't fair!

Tzu-hsi: Why not? I had it said to me at her age.

(*A clock chimes.*)

Kuang-Hsu: It is two o'clock by the clock which was given to me by the Czar of Russia.

Tzu-hsi: And what did you give him? Half of Manchuria?

(*Another clock chimes.*)

Kuang-Hsu: It is two o'clock by the clock given to me by the French premier—

Tzu-hsi: For which you gave his traders rights to the entire China Sea.

(*Another clock chimes.*)

Kuang-Hsu: It is two o'clock by the clock given to me by—

(Tzu-hsi *stops the pendulum of the clock that is chiming.*)

Tzu-hsi: *You* set the time! *You* regulate the hours for the empire! *You* determine the hours with the help of no other instrument but the sun!

Kuang-Hsu: Their clocks are exact—

Tzu-hsi: And every one is different! You betray your foolishness in thinking *they* hold the secret of time! The contrivances of their civilizations are mere toys against our art, our manners, our philosophy. These can be broken—(*She raises a hand as if to smash the clock.*)

Kuang-Hsu: No—!

TZU-HSI: But our ways *survive*.

(*She claps her hands.* SHEN TAI *enters, now very respectably dressed and groomed, very much her humble servant.*)

TZU-HSI: I introduce to you the renowned and highly skilled actor, Shen Tai, whom I have hired to give you Emperor lessons.

TUTOR: Emperor lessons!

TZU-HSI: You may be attempting to give him an Emperor's mind, but more to the point is that he learn how to walk and talk and carry himself as an Emperor. (*She turns to* KUANG-HSU.) Or do you think you already *are* like an Emperor?

KUANG-HSU: (*Humiliated*) No, Aunt.

TZU-HSI: Perhaps when Shen Tai finishes with you, you will actually be able to *rule*! (*She turns to* SHEN TAI.) Begin the lesson!

SHEN TAI: We'll start with the Emperor's walk. . . . An Emperor walks with his head up.

KUANG-HSU: Do it. I will copy you.

(SHEN TAI *demonstrates.* KUANG-HSU *tries it, not succeeding as well as* SHEN TAI.)

SHEN TAI: An Emperor walks with his shoulders back.

KUANG-HSU: I see.

(KUANG-HSU *tries it. He does not do it as well as* SHEN TAI.)

SHEN TAI: An Emperor carries himself like a god!

KUANG-HSU: I'll try . . .

(*The* PEARL CONCUBINE *approaches* SHEN TAI.)

PEARL: Where did you learn to walk like an Emperor?

SHEN TAI: I made it up. I am an actor. I can be anything, perform anything!

(SHEN TAI *does an acrobatic trick that ends with his land-ing on the throne.*)

TZU-HSI: *There* is an Emperor! Ask him to demonstrate any quality of a majestic leader.

KUANG-HSU: (*Considers for a moment, then:*) . . . Can you teach me—how the English do their waltz?

(TZU-HSI *throws up her hands, screams in frustration, and exits. The others exit, doing their very strange interpreta-tion of a waltz.*)

(*Lights change.*)

(*THE PALACE OF TRANQUIL OLD AGE.* TZU-HSI'S *au-dience chamber.*)

(*The General,* JUNG LU, *strides into the room. He is a strong, solid ex-soldier in his mid-sixties, a plain man with plain forceful thoughts.* LI *rushes in after him.*)

LI: How did you get past the outer gate?

JUNG LU: The guards recognized me. . . . I must speak to the Empress.

LI: Have you decided you are no longer banished? Perhaps she will not be of the same opinion.

JUNG LU: I am aware of the risk I run.

LI: She hasn't spoken your name in many years.

JUNG LU: I'm sure she has spoken yours often enough to make up for it.

LI: We are very intimate.

JUNG LU: A eunuch's intimacy!

LI: You stink, Jung Lu!

JUNG LU: At least my stink is the honest sweat of a long journey, while yours—

LI: Yes? Mine?

JUNG LU: Tell me, do you still carry your private parts in a bag around your waist so you won't reach heaven in a mutilated condition?

LI: You will one day get too frank, Jung Lu!

JUNG LU: It was what she valued most about me.

LI: Stolid and devoted as ever!

JUNG LU: Yes.

LI: Then how could you have betrayed her in the bed of an inferior?

JUNG LU: That is a long time past now.

LI: It may not be past for the Empress.

(*Silence. To this,* JUNG LU *has no rejoinder. At last he says:*)

JUNG LU: How much do you want for arranging to let me see her?

LI: I am Keeper of the Treasury. What more could I want?

JUNG LU: You *always* want more!

LI: Yes. That is the joy of wealth. Unlike desire for sex, desire for wealth can never be sated.

JUNG LU: Name your price. I have not travelled six days to stand outside her chamber!

LI: I will take—the knife she gave you.

JUNG LU: The knife—

LI: What use is it to a general without an army?

(JUNG LU *touches the jewelled knife at his waist, hesitating.*)

Don't tell me you have a sentimental attachment to it!

(TZU-HSI *suddenly appears.*)

TZU-HSI: Such sentiment would be ill-advised.

JUNG LU: Empress—!

TZU-HSI: I will take the knife. After all, the audience is with me, is it not?

(*He hands her the knife. Coolly, she hands it over to* LI.)

TZU-HSI: I reward fidelity.

JUNG LU: (*Bowing deeply*) Empress—

TZU-HSI: Do not patronize me with pretended humility!

JUNG LU: (*Rising*) Are you well?

TZU-HSI: Love is the only incurable disease, and I am blessed never to have been afflicted.

JUNG LU: It is your privilege, if you wish, to rewrite the past.

TZU-HSI: Every other person is a prison. . . . Why have you intruded yourself into my presence?

JUNG LU: I—

TZU-HSI: You are flabby, by the way.

JUNG LU: And greying. But still faithful.

TZU-HSI: If you presume I wish you to be faithful, you presume too much!

JUNG LU: Empress, I know you as no other man has known you—

TZU-HSI: Arrogant!

JUNG LU: Before you were sixteen, you were secluded in your father's house. Since you were sixteen, you have hardly been outside these walls.

TZU-HSI: I know the story of my life!

JUNG LU: Walled up in this palace, one's view of the world can become distorted—

TZU-HSI: On the contrary. A distance from the world can bring perspective.

JUNG LU: In a way, for me, my banishment has been a boon.

TZU-HSI: For me, a blessing!

JUNG LU: It let me see things. Let me travel in the country. And I come to you now, myself—because I am the only one who has ever dared to bring you bad news.

TSU-HSI: This man is not to be borne! He happily absented himself for years! And now he returns to give me the tribute of announcing disaster! I will not listen!

JUNG LU: Empress, your fate is intimately tied to the fate of the country. And the country is ill, deeply ill.

TZU-HSI: And so would you be, if you had foreign soldiers stationed on your soil and could not get rid of them! So would you be if the heavens sent disease and famine, and your enemies sent greedy traders, wily missionaries—

JUNG LU: Why do our people listen to the missionaries? Because the missionaries feed them! I have seen a man sell his soul for a bowl of soup! I have seen others sell their daughters for a dram of opium! You have a country *drugged*—because it is too horrifying to be awake! If only you could *see* your people—

TZU-HSI: Do you make a religion of suffering humanity? Is a man good because he suffers?

JUNG LU: Suffering makes him angry.

TZU-HSI: Fine! In anger is energy! In energy is hope!

JUNG LU: It makes him wild.

TZU-HSI: Exactly the kind of man I like!

JUNG LU: Why do you joke?

TZU-HSI: Because you come here full of news and tell me nothing I do not already know!

JUNG LU: You know, but you don't *see*! Try to see what lies beyond these walls. See—hordes of bandits roaming the countryside. A savage force, neither a part of us nor a part of the West. They wear red headbands. They call themselves The Society of Righteous and Harmonious Fists. The English call them the Boxers.

They are fanatics, bound in secret societies. Obsessed with rituals, spells and incantations. They claim to be able to live through the hail of bullets! I myself have seen them pass swords through their palms and not bleed!

Jung Lu: "They claim to be able to live through the hail of bullets! I myself have seen them pass swords through their palms and not bleed!" (Jung Lu: Ray Dooley, and Boxers, from the Cincinnati production (Illusion #2, The Boxer Threat). Photo copyright 1984 by Sandy Underwood.)

They prey on missionaries, traders, and anyone else they like. And the viceroys can do nothing, because the people believe in them and protect them.

TZU-HSI: And so should I—if they could live through bullets!

JUNG LU: Empress, it's this new danger I've come to tell you about. There is a spirit of rebellion—

TZU-HSI: The Drum of Remonstrance stands in the palace courtyard—to be sounded in protest against a house which is unworthy to rule. In the three hundred years of this Dynasty, that drum has never even been approached! The Ch'ing Dynasty still possesses the Mandate of Heaven.

JUNG LU: For how long?

TZU-HSI: China has been through times of disaster before. They are decreed by Heaven—as a cleansing process.

Afterwards, the country and the Dragon Throne will be stronger than ever.

JUNG LU: I have warned you—

TZU-HSI: Go back and cultivate your lilies.

JUNG LU: Something must be done!

TZU-HSI: Some things have changed since you left, don't you realize? I am no longer Regent. My nephew is on the throne. I have no say. I devote myself to my mulberry trees, my water picnics.

JUNG LU: You must act!

TZU-HSI: I am not in power!

JUNG LU: (*Steadily*) The day you cease to be in power will be the day you cease to live.

(*Their eyes meet, piercingly.*)

(*Lights change.*)

(*THE HALL OF SUPREME HARMONY. The* TUTOR *shows a group of documents to* KUANG-HSU *as the* PEARL *looks on.*)

TUTOR: These decrees will bring China into the modern era—

KUANG-HSU: My aunt will never allow me to sign them.

TUTOR: She doesn't need to know—

KUANG-HSU: She has the right to see every decree I publish!

PEARL: Yes. But the law says nothing about *when.*

KUANG-HSU: Still, I—

TUTOR: Emperor, the people are crying out for help! You can change the ways of centuries—just by putting characters on parchment and affixing your official seal!

(KUANG-HSU *turns to the* PEARL.)

KUANG-HSU: Do you think I can?

PEARL: I think you can work miracles.

KUANG-HSU: Then yes. I want to try. (*He opens the decrees one by one.*) By this decree, I set up a commission to study giving the people the right to vote and a constitution. By this, I declare the barbarous practice of footbinding to be forever outlawed in this land. By this, I establish schools to teach science and engineering.

TUTOR: By this, you encourage free speech—

KUANG-HSU: Will my people be able to talk to me directly? Face to face?

TUTOR: It will be encouraged.

KUANG-HSU: And will I be able to go out and see them?

TUTOR: Your best witness is your own eyes.

KUANG-HSU: Mine and my Pearl's.

PEARL: We'll travel through the provinces together—

KUANG-HSU: By train!

TUTOR: And there's something else. Something you must see to personally.

KUANG-HSU: Anything!

TUTOR: You must have a son.

(PEARL *and* KUANG-HSU *exchange a look.*)

KUANG-HSU: You sound just like my aunt!

TUTOR: Does this request seem indelicate from me? I'm sorry. I have my dreams for China's future—and yet, I know the ways of her people are rooted in the past. There would be no faster way for you to ensure their loyalty and love than by giving them a son.

KUANG-HSU: Do you think one can create a child by decree, the way one can create a railroad?

(SHEN TAI *enters.* PEARL *greets him extravagantly, to save* KUANG-HSU's *emotional response.*)

PEARL: Look! Here is Shen Tai, come to continue your Emperor lessons! How is the Emperor progressing, Shen Tai?

SHEN TAI: Imperially!

PEARL: Shen Tai was telling me all about his life the other day. He was once almost eaten by a wolf.

SHEN TAI: But I ate him first.

PEARL: Shen Tai is very resourceful.

KUANG-HSU: I hope to make it unnecessary forever for my people to dine on wolves. . . . What are you going to teach me today?

SHEN TAI: How to strengthen your voice.

KUANG-HSU: Well, that's a beginning—

SHEN TAI: We take the voice from the nose—and place it in the chest, thus—

(*He intones a sound through the nose, then lowers it deeply into the chest.* KUANG-HSU *tries it, but cannot manage the lower register. The effect is comic.*)

SHEN TAI: Perhaps it would be better with words.

(*Before anyone can stop him, he picks up one of the decrees and begins to read aloud:*)

SHEN TAI: "I, the Kuang-Hsu Emperor, decree that the universities shall teach the Western sciences of—"

(*The* TUTOR *snatches the secret document from his hand.*)

TUTOR: Extemporize!

(*In a very deep voice,* SHEN TAI *begins swiftly and nervously to extemporize:*)

SHEN TAI: I, the Kuang-Hsu Emperor, the Fatherly, Auspicious, Heaven-Blessed, Brightly Manifest, Calm, Sedate, Perfect—

(KUANG-HSU, *attempting the majestic low voice, repeats:*)

KUANG-HSU: "Calm, sedate, perfect—" (*Suddenly he cuts off and cries out*:) It does not sound like me!

(*Lights change.*)

(*THE GARDEN. As* LI *stands in the background, the* WIFE *sits on a bench holding a basket of paper flowers.* TZU-HSI *is attaching them one by one to the bare branch of a tree.*)

TZU-HSI: In all the world, I am the only one to have peach blossoms in February!

WIFE: This is true, Empress. . . . But what if it rains?

TZU-HSI: Then you'll make new ones! The weather serves *us*, we do not serve *her*! Nature must be forced.

WIFE: I learn so much from you.

TZU-HSI: And from you I learn so little! You were supposed to tell me everything that happens in your husband's quarters.

WIFE: But I see him so seldom! He works in secret with his tutor all day long and late into each evening.

TZU-HSI: And on what—on *what*—are they expending these tremendous labors?

WIFE: I do not know. I am not in his confidence.

TZU-HSI: You do, sometimes, do you not, share his bed?

WIFE: Not as often as I should. The Pearl Concubine has so ensnared him—

TZU-HSI: Then you must work to ensnare him even more!

WIFE: I don't know how!

TZU-HSI: I have no time to give you lessons in pleasure at this moment! I do not care about your pleasure-or his. I want only to know his mind—his *mind*—and you can penetrate that through his senses.

WIFE: I will do whatever you tell me.

TZU-HSI: A man is at your mercy twice—when his desire is high and when his desire is sated. When desire is flaming in him, discretion vanishes. He does not know what he is saying, does not care. Withhold your favors until he rises to a madness. Then any secret that he has is yours. . . . Or, if madness rules and words become impossible, then wait until after the act, after the final shudder. When his seed is spent and his body begs for rest, then he is off his guard. Then, too, you can coax his inner mind to speak to you.

WIFE: Yes, Empress.

TZU-HSI: Then you understand?

WIFE: Yes, Empress. Only one thing—

TZU-HSI: Yes?

WIFE: What is this "final shudder" of which you speak?

(TZU-HSI *stares at her.*)

TZU-HSI: Repeat the question.

WIFE: I should like to know what it is so I may recognize it and follow your instructions when it happens.

TZU-HSI: Then you do not know?

WIFE: No, Empress. It is something I have never witnessed.

TZU-HSI: When you go to the Emperor's bed, what do you do there?

WIFE: I am not chosen often.

TZU-HSI: When you *are* chosen, what do you do?

WIFE: I am carried there. I lie subject to his mouth and fingers. When he falls asleep, I am carried out.

TZU-HSI: And that is all? That is *all*?

WIFE: What else should there be?

(TZU-HSI *screams in rage. Stunned, the* WIFE *begins to sob.*)

How have I failed to please you?

TZU-HSI: Must I always be surrounded by innocence and ugliness?! Leave my sight!

(*Sobbing, the* WIFE *runs out.* TZU-HSI *breaks out in wild, ironic laughter.* LI *joins in heartily.*)

TZU-HSI: She is a virgin! The wife I personally planted in the Emperor's bed remains an unviolated little girl! She might as well have been sleeping with you!

LI: Does his impotence surprise you?

TZU-HSI: I suspected it. But the Pearl Concubine looks so content—!

LI: Perhaps her contentment is based on something else — like "true love".

TZU-HSI: How revolting!

LI: (*Smiling*) The unfortunate Emperor must be suffering the effects of his dissolute youth.

TZU-HSI: All of which he spent in your company! I can imagine how you must have enjoyed watching him on the pleasure barges and in the opium dens of this city.

LI: I had to see he was entertained during your regency. Especially when you insisted on extending your regency for so inordinate a time.

TZU-HSI: He was an infant until way past his majority. I sometimes think he needs a wet nurse now! China has been unfortunate in her males.

LI: But supremely fortunate in you. How blessed we are that there appeared a female gifted with your qualities.

TZU-HSI: Gifted! It was no gift, it was the me I *made*! . . . When I first came to the palace, I was ready to be the perfect feminine complement to my masculine lord. And then there came those nights in my master's bed. His fears, his inabilities, his weeping! And the impotence of his nights was nothing compared to the impotence of his days!

One night I had a dream. I was in a chariot being driven by my husband. We were racing down a mountainside at the speed of the wind! Fast, ever faster, the horses hurtled forward! We were out of control! I cried out to my husband to rein the horses in! He sat transfixed, he could do nothing! In another moment we would plummet over the precipice! I grabbed the reins. I took control. I saved the chariot! *I* kept the country on its path. *I*. Not him. When there was a decision to be made, I made it. When there was a son to be made, I made that, too. Where are the women today who would dare what I dared? They do not exist!

(*Lights change.*)

(*THE EMPTY CHAMBER. Night. The prison has become* SHEN TAI'S *room. The instruments of torture, while still there, have been pushed aside. At the moment,* SHEN TAI *is burrowing deep into the trunk, trying on costume after costume. He comes up with an elaborate piece of warrior's armor and proudly dons it. He is delighted with himself.*)

SHEN TAI: If only my friends could see me! I am actually living in the palace! I—humble I—am permitted to look upon the Empress's face! I give lessons to the Emperor. And I'm better at playing his part than he is! Who knows how far I might rise if I do all the Empress expects of me? What a stroke of fortune! What more could a poor peasant ask?

(*He turns. The* PEARL CONCUBINE *has slipped quietly into his chamber.* SHEN TAI *is astounded.*)

You! Here?

(*The* PEARL CONCUBINE *is nervous but determined. She has come on a mission. She will get it done.*)

PEARL: I came—to thank you for your instruction of the Emperor.

SHEN TAI: Oh, don't mention it—(*Then, when she doesn't speak.*) He is progressing well, don't you think?

PEARL: Very well.

SHEN TAI: Next, I'm going to teach him how to lead his troops into battle!

PEARL: That could be—a very useful lesson. . . . I have no way to show my gratitude.

SHEN TAI: No need. No need at all. . . . Actually, I'm surprised you're here. I wouldn't think you'd even notice me.

PEARL: Not notice you! When you're the only man in the compound?

SHEN TAI: What about the tutor?

PEARL: He is not allowed to stay the night. Three thousand eunuchs—and you're the only male allowed to spend the night within the walls!

SHEN TAI: That must be very hard on all the concubines.

PEARL: Very. Our turns in the Emperor's bed come up so seldom.

SHEN TAI: But you're the favorite. Your turn must come up often.

PEARL: Often—(*She hesitates, then says it.*)—but not often enough.

SHEN TAI: (*Sympathetically*) Oh. (*Then suddenly he understands.*) Oh! (*He grins*) So that's why you're here! . . . Well, if it's a good time you want—!

(*He moves toward her. Instinctively, she moves back, then remembers her resolve.*)

PEARL: Yes. A good time.

SHEN TAI: I'll see that you get it!

(*He grabs her roughly. It frightens her. She holds him away.*)

PEARL: You are—well? You are not—impure? You are strong, and know, perhaps, that you could even be a—father?

SHEN TAI: Ask the girls in Shantung province.

PEARL: I will trust your word.

SHEN TAI: (*Confidentially*) The Emperor's not much of a love maker, is he?

PEARL: I will hear no criticism of my lord!

SHEN TAI: All right, all right, no criticism! But I'll show you what it's like to be made love to by a real man!

(*He grabs her purposefully. She is frightened.*)

PEARL: Wait! One moment!

SHEN TAI: What do you mean, one moment! It'll be too late in one moment!

(*He grabs her firmly and begins to make love to her. She cries out.*)

SHEN TAI: What's the matter with you?

PEARL: Nothing.

SHEN TAI: *You* came to *me*, remember?

PEARL: I remember. (*Remembering her resolve, she girds herself for his advances.*)

SHEN TAI: Well, go ahead. Cry out if you want to. If you'll enjoy it better. I heard about you concubines. You pretend to lose your maidenheads every time! (*Roughly, he lays her down.*)

(*Lights change.*)

(*THE PALACE OF TRANQUIL OLD AGE.* LI *hurries in and hands* TZU-HSI *a document.*)

LI: Empress—

TZU-HSI: So this is the document my nephew and his tutor have been working on for months in secret! (*She opens the exceedingly long decree and bursts out laughing.*) I have never read anything so amusing in my life! My nephew thinks he will establish the Celestial Kingdom on Earth with one stroke of his pen! . . . Why doesn't he just rename China 'Europe' and be done with it! (*She throws the endless document to the floor.*) Idealistic garbage! Tell him I shall not let him make a fool of himself by making these provisions public!

LI: (*Folding up the decree*) Empress, you know by law you have the right to *see* every document the Emperor publishes, but not the right to take action.

TZU-HSI: My advice is action enough. He has the spine of a jellyfish.

LI: It seems the jellyfish has developed a backbone.

TZU-HSI: What do you mean?

LI: These reforms went into effect today.

TZU-HSI: Without my knowledge or consent?!

LI: Your nephew had them sent to all the provinces two weeks ago. They were sealed, with instructions to open them this morning.

TZU-HSI: The very moment they were sent to me?

LI: Exactly.

TZU-HSI: How dare he—! (*She sputters in rage.*) This is a deliberate act of his against me!

LI: But still within the law. Exactly within the letter of the law.

TZU-HSI: I know these tricks! He cannot play them as well as I! . . . Why didn't you tell me?

LI: I only discovered it this morning, when some viceroys asked for clarifications—

TZU-HSI: This insolence could not be his own idea.

LI: I agree. He would have to be led.

TZU-HSI: His tutor—

LI: Yes. I'm certain.

TZU-HSI: Summon him to me!

LI: I have taken that liberty. He is just outside. (*He claps his hands.*)

TZU-HSI: How well you know my mind, Li. Can you guess what I have in store for him?

LI: I am eager to see it.

(*The* TUTOR *enters and bows politely. He feels confident and sure of himself.*)

TZU-HSI: I have read—the Emperor's—new edicts. They are immensely edifying.

TUTOR: They are meant to be.

TZU-HSI: So we are to study all the ways of the West and do all we can to imitate them?

TUTOR: We shall take advantage of all they have discovered.

TZU-HSI: And shall we have our eyes rounded and our skin painted chalk white?

TUTOR: We shall take what applies and adapt it for our own usage.

TZU-HSI: Are you a prophet?

TUTOR: An historian.

TZU-HSI: Do you know everything?

TUTOR: Enough to help me see.

TZU-HSI: What did I have for breakfast?

TUTOR: I do not know.

TZU-HSI: And he claims to be a font of wisdom! Mark him down, Li!

(LI *brushes a character on parchment.*)

TUTOR: I know the temper of the people—

TZU-HSI: How old is this chrysanthemum?

TUTOR: (*Annoyed at her irrelevant questions.*) Three days.

TZU-HSI: Three hundred *years*! It has gone from seed to plant to seed to plant for three whole centuries! Mark him down, Li!

(LI *makes another mark.*)

TUTOR: The answer depends on whether one takes the long view or the short view—

TZU-HSI: Does it? And does that apply not only to flowers but to civilizations?

TUTOR: Yes, of course—

TZU-HSI: What color is my hair?

TUTOR: Why are you asking me these ridiculous questions?

TZU-HSI: What color is my hair?

(*He looks at her raven locks and considers the meaning of the question. Then he answers:*)

TUTOR: Your hair is white.

TZU-HSI: Does this look white to you?

TUTOR: You meant what color is it really!

TZU-HSI: I meant what color do you *see*! You have not the wisdom of a child! Mark him down!

(LI *does so.*)

TUTOR: You are trying to trap me!

TZU-HSI: As the West is trying to trap China! You cannot borrow their ways without having them possess our minds!

TUTOR: They believe in the good of the greatest number—

TZU-HSI: That is nonsense.

TUTOR: They believe in happiness for the common man—

TZU-HSI: They are deluded.

TUTOR: They believe in equality for all—

TZU-HSI: They are stupid! Humans are not equal to each other. They never shall be! There are the wise and the foolish, there are the noble and the debased. Out of what misguided sentimentality can you believe that the noble ones must constantly lower themselves to cater to the welfare of the mob? Must we constantly be looking down? Is it not for them to look up—and do their best to follow?

TUTOR: Our people are dying—

TZU-HSI: So they are. And in good conscience we must accept the sacrifice of those who must suffer in order to bring society to a higher state of being.

TUTOR: That is abomination!

TZU-HSI: It is truth. When will you idealists free yourselves from your maudlin romanticism about the "little people"? What seems abomination on the level of the individual is the highest morality on the level of the state.

TUTOR: You have no faith in goodness—

TZU-HSI: Goodness is cowardice.

TUTOR: You have no faith in progess—

TZU-HSI: I am proud of from whence I have come.

TUTOR: And what is to be? A country overrun by savages in red headbands?

TZU-HSI: If they will free us of the foreigners.

TUTOR: We will never be free of the foreigners. That time is over! What is at stake is the survival of China!

TUTOR: *I* will decide what is best for the survival of China!

TUTOR: May I remind you that it is your *nephew* who is on the throne!

(*An icy pause, then* TZU-HSI *says, exceedingly calmly:*)

TZU-HSI: Are you shouting at me?

TUTOR: I am trying to make you understand—!

TZU-HSI: Li, he was shouting.

(LI *begins to write.*)

TUTOR: I care as much as you care—

TZU-HSI: (*Sweetly*) Do you know you can be banished from the land for shouting in the Imperial Presence?

TUTOR: You are joking.

TZU-HSI: I am not joking. I hereby banish you for shouting.

TUTOR: There is no such law!

TZU-HSI: There is.

(*She signs her name to the paper* LI *has been writing.*)

TUTOR: The ink on that edict is not yet dry!

TZU-HSI: It is as dry as the ink on yours. And just as valid. You underestimate me. My brain is not white. My brain is as black as the color of my hair. You do not know how black my brain is! . . . You are unfit to be a tutor and unfit to remain in this land. Go! Do not attempt to see the Emperor. From the moment you leave my sight, your life is in peril! Go!

(*The* TUTOR *bows and goes.*)

Did you see him go cold? What a battle! It was almost like flogging him! Almost as satisfying!

(*She claps her hands.* SHEN TAI *enters and bows deeply.*)

Why did you not inform me of the edicts which were being drawn up in my nephew's chambers?

SHEN TAI: I did not know—

TZU-HSI: It was your duty to know. It is the reason you were put there! It is the reason I bothered to spare your life.

SHEN TAI: They worked in greatest secrecy—

TZU-HSI: You have not been tortured in weeks, perhaps you miss it!

SHEN TAI: No, Empress.

TZU-HSI: Perhaps you want to perform for me.

SHEN TAI: Yes! Of course! I do!

TZU-HSI: Perform!

SHEN TAI: What do you want to see?

TZU-HSI: Those heroes in red headbands.

SHEN TAI: The ones the foreigners call the Boxers?

TZU-HSI: I understand they are invincible.

SHEN TAI: Yes, Empress.

TZU-HSI: I understand they can pass knives through their palms without bleeding.

SHEN TAI: Yes, Empress.

TZU-HSI: Show me this trick.

SHEN TAI: But I am not a Boxer!

TZU-HSI: You are what I say you are! Show me!

SHEN TAI: Yes, Empress.

(TZU-HSI *holds out her hand and* LI *gives her the jewelled knife. She hands it to* SHEN TAI *who holds it, trembling.*)

First they put themselves into a trance—

TZU-HSI: I have no time for trances!

SHEN TAI: They whirl around three times—

TZU-HSI: No whirling! Show me what I want to see!

SHEN TAI: They make themselves impervious to pain—

TZU-HSI: I tell you, *show me!*

(*He closes his eyes and stabs himself through his palm. He cries out in agony.*)

You must not cry out! Again!

(*He stabs himself again, stifling his cries although the pain is excruciating. The blood begins to flow.*)

And you must not bleed! Again! Again! Again!

(*In agony he stabs himself again and again as the blood flows profusely. She revels in his pain, with almost sexual enjoyment.*)

(*Lights change.*)

(*THE GARDEN. A sunny day.* KUANG-HSU *and* PEARL *are playing a game on a marble board.* KUANG-HSU *plays and wins. He laughs.*)

PEARL: You win again!

KUANG-HSU: I feel lucky. Do you know—weeks have passed and Aunt hasn't dared confront me! This time I have out-manoeuvred her!

PEARL: Why haven't you heard from your tutor?

KUANG-HSU: He must be in the provinces, carrying out my decrees. Come, let's have a picnic on Aunt's artificial lake! We'll take my new motorized boat and cruise out to the Ocean Terrace—

PEARL: No, Kuang-Hsu—

KUANG-HSU: What's the matter?

PEARL: I am—uneasy—near this lake of hers.

KUANG-HSU: You, who fear nothing, fear the lake?

PEARL: Last night I dreamed of a woman who drowned trying to embrace the reflection of her child in the water—

KUANG-HSU: Phantoms! Superstitions! I'll protect you!

PEARL: Do you fear nothing?

KUANG-HSU: Not any more! Oh, Pearl, I myself am going to bring China triumphant into this next century! Who would have thought I could accomplish this! For the first time in my life, I feel strong! I feel—manly! I feel—at this moment—I could even make love . . .

(*He comes to her. She whispers.*)

PEARL: Oh, try, my love. Please try . . .

(*They embrace.*)

(*Lights change.*)

(*THE EMPTY CHAMBER. Night.* SHEN TAI *lies asleep on his mat. His hand is bandaged. Every time he moves he moans in his sleep. After a moment, a figure silently appears. It is the* TUTOR. *His face and clothing bear marks of the fugitive life which, in the past weeks, he has lived.* SHEN TAI *stirs and wakens with a start.*)

SHEN TAI: Who is here?

TUTOR: Don't be afraid—

SHEN TAI: You! How can you be here? You have been banished!

TUTOR: What can I achieve outside the borders of the country?

SHEN TAI: But here you are in danger—

(*He moves and in doing so hurts his injured hand, which makes him cry out.*)

TUTOR: What have they done to you?

SHEN TAI: Nothing.

TUTOR: That doesn't look like nothing.

SHEN TAI: I did it to myself. She said do it—and I did it! I almost believed it wouldn't bleed, wouldn't hurt! . . . How could I have done such a thing?

TUTOR: It's *her*. She holds all China in her prison chamber! Nothing will release us from that bondage—except her death.

SHEN TAI: I think she plans to live forever.

TUTOR: Many who have had such plans—have found themselves deceived.

SHEN TAI: In a play, words like that would have dark mysterious significance.

TUTOR: And in life, my friend—in life?

(SHEN TAI *looks at him in amazement. The* TUTOR *goes on:*)

Listen to me. I am a scholar. I have spent all my life with books. I thought all things could be achieved by good actions and good thoughts, by debate, by reason. But now I know: there is no place for reason while she is alive to act against it. She is the great disease from which the country must be cured!

SHEN TAI: Do I hear what I hear? I think you mean *murder*!

TUTOR: *Deliverance.* The entire country is waiting to be released—and you are the sword.

SHEN TAI: Me!

TUTOR: You are the only one who has access to her.

SHEN TAI: I can't.

TUTOR: You have played murderers—

SHEN TAI: But afterwards the victims get up!

TUTOR: And will the Emperor get up if she wills otherwise?

SHEN TAI: But he's her nephew!

TUTOR: And once she had a son . . .

(*Silence. Then* SHEN TAI *cries out:*)

SHEN TAI: I can't—! I can't—!

(*He makes a violent gesture and in doing so disturbs his injury. He cradles his hand. Quietly, the* TUTOR *says:*)

TUTOR: Have you ever seen the remnants of a man who is no longer a man?

(*Slowly he pulls aside his robe and shows his mutilation.* SHEN TAI *stares in horror.*)

She said I was only banished. But her men were waiting outside the walls.

SHEN TAI: Horrible—

TUTOR: This is what she does to us. To us all. She mutilates our country. For our *country*—for *China*. You *must*—

(SHEN TAI *stares at him.*)

I have a plan, Shen Tai. It cannot fail . . .

(*Lights change.*)

(*THE PALACE OF TRANQUIL OLD AGE. Night.* TZU-HSI *is examining herself in a hand mirror. Her hair, unpinned for the night, falls black and straight to a length lower than her waist. After several moments, the* WIFE *enters.*)

TZU-HSI: You're late!

WIFE: I wasn't sure you'd still want me to come. You seemed so displeased with me—

TZU-HSI: No one else does my hair as well as you do. If it's your one skill, I don't see why I shouldn't take advantage of it.

(*The* WIFE *begins to brush. Suddenly* TZU-HSI *cries out:*)

Ow! You've pulled out a strand! Put it back! Put it back!

(*Nonplussed, the* WIFE *stands holding the offending strand for a moment. Then, obediently, she tries to put it back into* TZU-HSI's *hair.*)

What's the matter? Do you think I am too vain?

WIFE: No, Empress.

TZU-HSI: The body is the house in which the soul lives. We must take infinite care of the body.

WIFE: Then you'll be happy to hear the news I have to tell you. I passed Shen Tai on my way in. He has a gift for you.

TZU-HSI: He has been negligent in his attentions to me lately.

WIFE: He says he'll share with you a secret of the actor's profession: a dye which will blacken the hair without blackening the scalp.

TZU-HSI: And he expects me to be grateful for such a gift? I who have the blackest hair in the entire country?! (*Then she adds diffidently:*) And the blackest scalp.

WIFE: He says the dye is so secret only he can administer it. He won't even let me watch.

TZU-HSI: Where is my new hair attendant?

WIFE: He said he would enter when you are alone.

TZU-HSI: Then leave me!

(*The* WIFE *exits.*)

I may as well pursue youth as assiduously as other old ladies.

(*Sitting in her high-backed chair,* TZU-HSI *studies her face in the mirror. It is here that she first glimpses* SHEN TAI *as he enters.*)

(SHEN TAI *is dressed exactly as* TZU-HSI *is dressed. The same robe, the same long nails, the same hair. He looks startlingly like her.*)

Well! What a costume for a hair attendant! ... Turn around! Turn around!

(*He does so.*)

Excellent. . . . Can you do my walk?

(*He walks*)

Can you do my voice?

SHEN TAI: (*In her voice*) "Well! What a costume for a hair attendant!"

TZU-HSI: Excellent! If you had my soul, you'd be me!

(SHEN TAI *begins to wrap her in a special protective cape he has brought with him. It goes over her shoulders, over the back of the chair, and down to her feet, covering her completely.*)

SHEN TAI: I have no desire to be you, Empress.

TZU-HSI: Truly? I thought the whole world must envy me.

SHEN TAI: Empress, after months of observing in the shadow of your presence, I am ready to present to you— the *true* story of your life.

TZU-HSI: So at last you think you know me.

SHEN TAI: Yes.

TZU-HSI: You haven't made me virtuous and boring?

SHEN TAI: No.

TZU-HSI: Well, then, let me see.

(*He moves across the room to begin.*)

What about my hair?

SHEN TAI: I will take care of it—at the end.

(*She sits back. Lights change.*)

(*Across the room,* SHEN TAI *begins, affecting her voice, her mannerisms. This time, his style is graceful and very creditable.*)

I am the Orchid Concubine, serene and beautiful. My lord is Emperor.

(*With movement and gesture, he pantomimes the Emperor.*)

TZU-HSI: Very good! Very good!

SHEN TAI: I present him with his only son! (*He pantomimes.*) My lord is happy. . . . But soon he dies. . . . I survive.

My son is named Emperor. He is still an infant. I am made co-regent with my husband's widow.

She is called the Empress of the East. I am called the Empress of the West.

TZU-HSI: I always hated that title.

SHEN TAI: My son grows—

My son marries—

After wiping his mouth with a certain napkin, my son is blessed with a visitation of the Heavenly Flowers. The smallpox! My son dies.

His pregnant wife throws herself into the nearest well.

I survive . . .

TZU-HSI: (*Without emotion*) My life abounds with tragedy.

SHEN TAI: I choose the new Emperor. A three-year-old. My nephew.

He prefers the Empress of the East.

The Empress of the East suffers a fatal attack of indigestion.

I survive.

(TZU-HSI *shifts in her chair but the cape holds her.*)

I am sole regent.

The Emperor grows.

I marry him to my niece.

He assumes the throne. . . .

Happy, I retire to the Palace of Tranquil Old Age.

TZU-HSI: What do you do there?

(*A pause. Then* SHEN TAI *takes a small vial from his pocket and says:*)

SHEN TAI: I think of taking my own life.

TZU-HSI: Now that would be an end to your play! Everyone loves a scene of dying. But *why* do you consider taking your own life?

SHEN TAI: Because I have plotted! I have lied! I have stolen power! I have murdered!

TZU-HSI: And you leave that out of your play? You are a fool, Shen Tai.

SHEN TAI: Whenever there was anyone in your way to power, they found themselves conveniently removed.

TZU-HSI: You are beginning to bore me!

(*The encumbering cape annoys her, but she cannot free herself from it. She realizes she is captive.*)

Why should I be afraid to take fate into my own hands? My hands are worthy. Not to act is cowardice. And I have never been afraid.

SHEN TAI: Not even now?

TZU-HSI: Go ahead! Dispatch me!

SHEN TAI: So many died!

TZU-HSI: Do you honor them for being innocent and dying? Death is a step up for them!

(*She looks at the vial.*)

Is that the hair dye?

SHEN TAI: A few drops anywhere on the skin—

TZU-HSI: Hurry, then! Do it! You will give me a great opportunity—

SHEN TAI: What opportunity?

TZU-HSI: To rule again, after my demise.

(*Puzzled at this, he stares at her, still holding the vial threateningly above her.*)

Surely you know that murdered spirits return to inhabit the bodies of their murderers. I shall come back as a demon inside you. You in my costume. You shall sit on the throne and I will reign another forty years!

SHEN TAI: The Kuang-Hsu Emperor will reign!

(*He comes to pour the liquid on her scalp. She throws back her head and laughs.*)

TZU-HSI: I wish you well in the reign of the Kuang-Hsu Emperor! Happy future in the dynasty of the joke! Do you wonder what has happened in the country since the Emperor's reforms went into effect? I'll tell you.

In Canton, the university has thousands of students signed up to learn the new subjects—but no one qualified to teach them. In Shanghai, where he reorganized the government, thousands of former employees are now out begging in the streets. In the interior, rather than help the foreigners lay tracks as they were ordered, workers threw themselves in front of the trains!

Everywhere there is chaos and confusion! Instead of curing the country's ills, the reforms have compounded them.

SHEN TAI: I had no idea—

(*She looks him squarely in the eye.*)

TZU-HSI: Heaven help this country when I die. It is *I* who for almost half a century have held it together! If you wonder where you can find the soul of this country, *I* am the soul of this country! In power or out of power, on the throne or off the throne, alive or dead, this country is *me*!

(SHEN TAI *falls to his knees before her.*)

SHEN TAI: Empress, I beg your forgiveness! You are supreme! Unsurpassable! All glorious! It is only that they are too blind to see!

TZU-HSI: Untie me, my twin, my other self. It is time, at last, for us to pay a visit to my devoted nephew.

(SHEN TAI *begins to release her.*)

(*Lights change.*)

(*THE HALL OF SUPREME HARMONY. Night* KUANG-HSU *is pacing aimlessly. The* PEARL CONCUBINE *tries to calm him.*)

KUANG-HSU: Within these walls I know nothing! Nothing! What is happening in the country? Why do I not hear one word!

PEARL: Can you not sleep?

KUANG-HSU: Something must have happened to my tutor. To send no messenger in all this time! And she—my aunt —says nothing. What is she thinking?

PEARL: It doesn't matter what she's thinking—

KUANG-HSU: I should have told her about my plans. I shouldn't have tried to act in secret. I cannot bear the silence any longer!

(TZU-HSI *enters, accompanied by* SHEN TAI, *who is still in her costume.*)

TZU-HSI: I am here, my nephew. And I bring you noise.

KUANG-HSU: Aunt—! Forgive me—

TZU-HSI: Forgive you? I congratulate you!

KUANG-HSU: Then you are no longer angry with me?

TZU-HSI: Angry with you? I am proud of you—for the first time in your life.

KUANG-HSU: I meant no harm—

TZU-HSI: Of course you didn't. What's a small assassination?

KUANG-HSU: Assassination!

TZU-HSI: Don't worry. Shen Tai confessed everything. I'm delighted by your cleverness. Yours and your tutor's.

KUANG-HSU: What has happened to my tutor?

TZU-HSI: Justice has happened to your tutor. I'm sure you don't mind.

KUANG-HSU: Are you saying he plotted your death?

TZU-HSI: Please, I want *you* to take all the credit—

KUANG-HSU: I knew nothing of this! Nothing! I would never plot against you—

TZU-HSI: If you had, I would have admired you.

KUANG-HSU: I would never—

TZU-HSI: I brought you up as my own son and this is how I am rewarded?

KUANG-HSU: No, Aunt—

TZU-HSI: Do you know the law of the Imperial Household for one who raises his hand against his mother?

(*She strikes him across the face. The* PEARL *cries out.*)

PEARL: Help! Guards!

(*No one enters.*)

TZU-HSI: It would seem you are without reinforcements. (*She gestures imperiously.*) Sit and write what I dictate to you.

KUANG-HSU: Whatever you say, Aunt. (*He sits on the throne and prepares to write.*)

TZU-HSI: (*Dictating*) "I, the Kuang-hsu Emperor, hereby revoke my former edicts—"

KUANG-HSU: No!

TZU-HSI: "Revoke my former edicts!"

(*Helplessly, he writes:*)

KUANG-HSU: "Revoke my former edicts . . ."

TZU-HSI: ". . . And establish, once again, our ancient and time-honored ways."

KUANG-HSU: ". . . Our ancient and time-honored ways . . ."

TZU-HSI: "Furthermore, for reasons of failing health, I find I am no longer able to carry on the task of being Emperor."

KUANG-HSU: No—!

TZU-HSI: If this plot against my life is revealed, you will be executed! I am giving you a chance to survive!

PEARL: You can't be so cruel—!

TZU-HSI: Stand away from him!

KUANG-HSU: (*Writing, feeling stunned and unreal*) "No longer able to carry on the task of being Emperor—" (*He stops*) I can't—! I can't—!

PEARL: How can you do this?

TZU-HSI: He is fortunate I am letting him live! . . . Why should you complain, you two? I am going to let you take up residence on the Ocean Terrace in the middle of the lake in the north garden. A lovely retreat. There, surrounded by water, you will be able to do anything you like—except leave.

(KUANG-HSU *is speechless. He and the* PEARL *look at each other. The* PEARL *says fiercely to* SHEN TAI:)

PEARL: If you were given the task of destroying her, why did you not do it?

(SHEN TAI *turns away from her.*)

TZU-HSI: Shen Tai is my loyal servant! (*Then she says:*) We must have witnesses! (*She cries out:*) Come, everyone! Bear witness!

(*From separate directions, the* WIFE, LI, *and* JUNG LU *arrive.*)

I want you all to witness a momentous occasion. In fact, it is so momentous, I want to witness it myself. Shen Tai, take my place!

(SHEN TAI *stands above* KUANG-HSU, *where* TZU-HSI *stood.* TZU-HSI *moves back to observe them.*)

Now, once more. Let me see this great moment.

(*She claps her hands.* SHEN TAI, *imitating* TZU-HSI, *dictates to* KUANG-HSU.)

SHEN TAI: Write what I dictate to you! . . . "I, the Kuang-hsu Emperor, hereby revoke my former edicts—"

(KUANG-HSU, *humiliated and upset, sits motionless.*)

TZU-HSI: (*To* SHEN TAI) Continue—

SHEN TAI: "Furthermore, for reasons of failing health, I find I am no longer able to carry on the task of being Emperor."

(LI *smiles and gives a congratulatory nod to* TZU-HSI.)

TZU-HSI: (*To* KUANG-HSU) Write!

KUANG-HSU: I have already written—(*He is weeping.*)

TZU-HSI: Well, then, write this—

(*With great satisfaction, she gestures to* SHEN TAI, *who pulls himself up imperiously to deliver this sentence in her voice, with her gestures.*)

SHEN TAI: "Unmindful of her age, my dear aunt has once more consented to take over the heavy burden of office—"

(KUANG-HSU *is unable to write. In* TZU-HSI'S *voice,* SHEN TAI *admonishes him.*)

Write, I said! "My dear aunt has once more consented to take over the heavy burden of office!"

(KUANG-HSU *breaks down weeping on the throne.* SHEN TAI, *as* TZU-HSI, *stand imperiously over him.*)

(TZU-HSI *applauds* SHEN TAI.)

TZU-HSI: I am magnificent!

(*She gestures* SHEN TAI *away and takes the place where he was standing. With her folded fan, she touches* KUANG-HSU *on the shoulder and firmly forces him to relinquish the throne. She takes her place before the throne and stands above the rest proudly. A gong sounds. Everyone bends in a deep kow-tow to her except* KUANG-HSU *and the* PEARL. *Tzu-HSI snaps her fan.* KUANG-HSU *grovels in deep kow-tow, pulling the* PEARL *down with him.* TZU-HSI *beams.*)

TZU-HSI: Magnificent!

(*With great satisfaction, she seats herself majestically on the throne.*)

BLACKOUT
END ACT ONE

ACT TWO

(*AT RISE: THE HALL OF SUPREME HARMONY. A golden auspicious dawn.*)

(*The Hall, which was once* KUANG-HSU'S *has become* TZU-HSI'S *and has increased in splendor. An Imperial Screen masks the throne.*)

(*A gong sounds. Followed by a procession of Servants,* LI *and* JUNG LU *enter from opposite sides and flank the Imperial Screen.* LI *wears an elaborate official robe.* JUNG LU *wears magnificent military regalia.*)

(*A gong sounds three times.* LI, JUNG LU, *and the Servants prostrate themselves in deep kow-tow.*)

(*Two Servants slowly pull away the Screen.* TZU-HSI *is revealed on the Dragon Throne in a magnificently embroidered robe.*)

(*All at once* KUANG-HSU'S *clocks begin to chime.* TZU-HSI *cries out:*)

TZU-HSI: Destroy those! The world will go on my time from now on!

(*The Servants remove the clocks and exit. From outside we hear the sound of the clocks being shattered.* TZU-HSI *smiles.*)

(TZU-HSI *claps her hands.* LI *and* JUNG LU *rise to a kneeling position. She smiles at them and says:*)

You never thought you'd see me up here, did you? I *told* you I was the cleverest woman alive! . . . Those who say absolute power corrupts obviously never had it.

LI: You are the most powerful woman in the world.

JUNG LU: Except, perhaps, for Queen Victoria.

TZU-HSI: Queen Victoria! The Queen of that tiny island? She's almost old enough to be my mother!

(JUNG LU *squirms. She commands:*)

Kneel at attention!

JUNG LU: I'm afraid my knees aren't what they used to be.

TZU-HSI: Truly? (*She smiles. Grandly she bestows a precedent-shattering boon:*) Very well. You may sit in my presence.

(LI *and* JUNG LU *look at her in astonishment.*)

I don't want it said I am not ready for the twentieth century.

(LI *and* JUNG LU *rise, then, very uncomfortably, take seats.*)

JUNG LU: If you're *really* ready for the new century, you'll agree to receive the British Ambassador.

LI: The throne does not speak to British!

JUNG LU: He has been chosen to speak for all the foreign delegations in Peking.

TZU-HSI: What are they complaining about now?

JUNG LU: A fresh outbreak of incidents against their nationals. Rail and telegraph lines cut. An English missionary murdered. A French priest tortured and killed.

TZU-HSI: If they were not here, they would not have these problems.

JUNG LU: And six more French nuns have been massacred.

LI: They were grinding up the eyes of Chinese children to use for medicines!

JUNG LU: Nonsense! The Boxers always have some excuse for their atrocities.

TZU-HSI: Was it the Boxers again? They are so patriotic.

JUNG LU: The dead foreigners don't think so.

TZU-HSI: Why don't the foreigners take their thoughts back to Europe where they belong?

JUNG LU: The legations would like to discuss these matters with you.

LI: The Empress cannot see them! They won't perform the kow-tow! They'll ask embarassing questions! They'll ask for forks! (*He pronounces* kow-tow *in the Chinese manner:* ker'-toe)

JUNG LU: You *must* receive Sir Claude MacDonald—

TZU-HSI: Did I say I wouldn't? (*She smiles. She calls out:*) Send in the British Ambassador!

(SHEN TAI, *gotten up like a British potentate, with sash and monocle, and looking like something out of* Pinafore, *pedals in smoking a cigar and riding a bicycle.*)

SHEN TAI: (*With an exaggerated British accent:*) I must have tea or I shall perish! (*He falls off the bicycle with a crash.*) Oh, my poor darling bicycle! My poor darling cigar!

TZU-HSI: Sir Claude, since you're down there already, you might as well perform the kow-tow. (*Pronounced* ker'-toe)

SHEN TAI: Oh, the kow-tow! The kow-tow! (*Howling with exaggerated British pronunciation.*) I simply cannot do it! (*He tries and drops his monocle.*)

TZU-HSI: Why have you come here, Sir Claude?

SHEN TAI: It's my duty to the heathen hordes. I absolutely positively *must* civilize you.

(*He hands* LI *a fork.* LI *sets it aside with extreme distaste.*)

TZU-HSI: Really? And how do you intend to do that?

SHEN TAI: By trade. . . . Would you like a little linsey-woolsey?

(*He pulls a length of homespun cloth from his pocket and tries to hand it to her. She pushes it away.*)

TZU-HSI: I have silk, what do I want with linsey-woolsey?

SHEN TAI: How about a little opium?

Shen Tai (as Sir Claude): "How about a little opium?" Tzu-hsi: "I prefer to stay awake." (Tzu-hsi: Ching Valdes; Shen Tai: Jonathan Fuller, from the Cincinnati production. Photo copyright 1984 by Sandy Underwood.)

(*He tries to give her a pipe.*)

TZU-HSI: I prefer to stay awake.

SHEN TAI: How about a little Christ? (*He pulls out a crucifix.*)

TZU-HSI: We have Buddha, thank you.

SHEN TAI: How can you be saved by someone who was such a fatty?

TZU-HSI: How can you be saved by someone who allowed himself to be hammered to death on two sticks?

SHEN TAI: But we have the One True Way. It is exceedingly generous on our part to share it with you.

Tzu-hsi: Actually, *we* have the One True Way.

SHEN TAI: You can't, my dear. You're yellow! . . . You can't be civilized until the day that you become White Christians.

TZU-HSI: White Christians! (*She rises.*) What you are saying is we should become prejudiced, intolerant, and despotic —like you.

(SHEN TAI *tries to speak.* TZU-HSI *silences him with an angry gesture.*)

Why should we talk to you? You think us barbarous, immoral, and uncivilized. You think us illiterate because all we speak is our own language!

You come here trying to make us into English. What if we did the same in reverse? What if we imported ten thousand British to work as cheap labor in our rice fields? What if we stationed Chinese troops in Piccadilly? What if we burned incense beneath the very nose of the Queen? What if we sent our priests to destroy your people's gods? Would you not do everything you could to get us out of your country?

(*She becomes deeply serious.*) A civilization of more than four thousand years is neither a child nor an imbecile! We are the land of Confucius and the three thousand mile wall. We are the land of grace, symmetry, peace, and wisdom. We are China. We were here long before you existed, and long after you are gone we shall remain.

(SHEN TAI *grovels on the floor in a deep kow-tow and, as Sir Claude, says:*)

SHEN TAI: Your majesty, your majesty—

TZU-HSI: Yes, Sir Claude?

SHEN TAI: Help me to become a Yellow Buddhist!

(*It is the climax of* SHEN TAI *and* TZU-HSI'S *prepared performance. She laughs in triumph.* LI *applauds enthusiastically.*)

LI: You were splendid, Empress!

JUNG LU: It's easy to be splendid when you've written your opponent's part for him. But how would you respond if the Ambassador said what he really came to say?

(JUNG LU *takes the sash from* SHEN TAI *and himself becomes the Ambassador—perhaps attempting a fusty old accent.*)

JUNG LU: Your Majesty—we are disturbed at the growing number of incidents against our nationals. It is not safe for us to be in your streets.

TZU-HSI: (*Enjoying the game*) Dear English Person: Why *are* you in our streets?

JUNG LU: Our presence here is recognized by law.

TZU-HSI: Laws are changing. *I* am on the throne now.

JUNG LU: By what authority?

TZU-HSI: (*Taken aback*) I beg your pardon?

JUNG LU: By what authority have you usurped the throne?

LI: Jung Lu, you go too far!

JUNG LU: I want to know by what right you reign in the reign of the Kuang-Hsu Emperor!

TZU-HSI: He was ill. He resigned voluntarily.

JUNG LU: Is he still alive?

LI: Are you accusing the Empress of murder?

JUNG LU: I'm asking what the foreigners would ask! . . . We want proof that he still exists! Nothing has been heard from him in many months.

TZU-HSI: Are you more interested in my nephew than in me?

JUNG LU: We have the right to deal with the legitimate ruler, and the legitimate ruler is not you!

(SHEN TAI *stares at this effrontery.* TZU-HSI *whirls on him.*)

Tzu-hsi: What are you gaping at? Take that contraption and get out of here!

(Shen Tai *takes the bicycle and hastily exits.*)

Li: (*To* Jung Lu) You have no right to address the Empress in this manner!

Jung Lu: The foreigners want to know you haven't dealt with Kuang-hsu treacherously so they can believe you won't deal with them treacherously.

Tzu-hsi: Do they see me as a double-headed dragon?

Jung Lu: They are afraid for their lives. They are begging you to provide them with armed protection against the Boxers!

Tzu-hsi: Do they expect me to send my own soldiers against my own people? Let them protect themselves—or get out! . . . They have ruined my day.

(*Lights change.*)

(*THE OCEAN TERRACE. The wall constantly reflect the surrounding water. All is delicate—like living within the shell of a pearly oyster. It is an incongruous prison—but a prison it is.*)

(Kuang-Hsu *is alone. On his knees, he stares at his image in the water and cries out to it in great self-hatred:*)

Kuang-Hsu: Fool! . . . Idiot! . . . Blunderer! . . . Is there anyone on Earth who can equal your stupidity! . . . Why did you try to act without her knowledge! Why did you give her cause to hate you? Why couldn't you have been strong?

(*He moves his hand furiously back and forth in the water as if trying to destroy his own image.*)

(*The* Pearl Concubine *enters with tea.*)

Kuang-Hsu: If I told my aunt from the beginning of the reforms I planned—

Pearl: She would never have allowed them to happen.

Kuang-Hsu: I never planned her *murder*—!

PEARL: She knows.

KUANG-HSU: How could my tutor have gone ahead—

PEARL: He should never have entrusted the deed to that absurd actor who now fawns all over your aunt. A man so fickle! So easily swayed—

KUANG-HSU: *I* was the greatest fool.

PEARL: You can't go over and over this . . .

KUANG-HSU: All my plans! All my glorious plans!

PEARL: Someday they will all come to pass—you'll see.

KUANG-HSU: (*Tortured*) Where is the Eunuch?

PEARL: He has not yet come.

KUANG-HSU: Each day he comes later and later!

PEARL: It only seems so. Drink your tea.

KUANG-HSU: Where is he?

PEARL: Can you not rest?

KUANG-HSU: Where *is* he?

(*He paces, distraught, breaking out in a cold sweat, beginning to show the effect of his opium dependence. His* WIFE *enters.*)

WIFE: What a lovely ride I've just had on the lake! Pity you're not allowed it.

PEARL: I don't know why you continue to address him. He has refused to speak one word to you since the day we were placed on this island.

WIFE: I address him because, although he is practically out of his mind, he is not deaf. I address him because he hears everything I say!

KUANG-HSU: Get her away! Get her away! She is only here to report my every breath to my aunt!

WIFE: Oh, are you still breathing?

KUANG-HSU: (*Singing wildly to block her voice from his head.*) "There was an Emperor who had a shrew for a wife, a shrew for a wife. And he shut his head to her, for the rest of his life, the rest of his life—"

(LI *enters.*)

LI: The sounds that come from this island are delicious! Like the quacking of wild geese!

KUANG-HSU: You are late!

LI: I am not aware that we have any set time—or even that I have any obligation to come here.

KUANG-HSU: Have you brought it?

LI: Prison life has made you indelicate.

KUANG-HSU: Have you brought my pipe?

(LI *smiles enigmatically.*)

PEARL: Answer him!

LI: (*Not answering*) Your aunt sends her felicitations—

KUANG-HSU: Is she coming to see me?

LI: She misses your splendid face. She has asked me to take your photograph.

(*Servants enter with a box camera on a tripod.*)

PEARL: I can imagine how much she craves to see his face!

KUANG-HSU: Oh, let me see! (*He examines the camera eagerly.*) There should be a silver-coated plate. And when I look in here, everything will be upside down. . . . Oh yes. It's wonderful!

LI: If you'll stand in the light—

PEARL: Don't do it. Don't play into her hands. If you pose for him you give a sign to the world that you consent to your intolerable imprisonment.

(KUANG-HSU *looks at her, then says to* LI:)

KUANG-HSU: I must refuse to have my photograph taken.

LI: You want your pipe . . .

(KUANG-HSU *realizes he must obey. He stands weak and wide-eyed while* LI *focusses the camera.*)

Smile. You don't want the world to see the Emperor looking cross and petulant.

(KUANG-HSU *attempts to smile.* LI *takes the picture.*)

WIFE: I don't think the world will be impressed. (*She goes out.*)

(KUANG-HSU *holds out his hand. With a slight smile,* LI *hands him the pipe.*)

PEARL: (*To* LI) This has been your way from the start—to corrupt him with pleasures.

LI: Only a woman can corrupt a man so deeply.

KUANG-HSU: There's nothing in this pipe!

(LI *smiles and, with infinite slowness, produces a small sack of opium from his pocket.* KUANG-HSU *snatches it and packs it into his pipe.*)

PEARL: How you enjoy his pain, you and she! Watching it is your greatest pleasure!

LI: Why shouldn't he give me pleasure? I give pleasure to him.

PEARL: You are a demon!

LI: (*Lighting* KUANG-HSU'S *pipe.*) Your master does not seem to think so.

(KUANG-HSU *lies back with his pipe, satisfied.* LI *exits.*)

(PEARL *arranges the pillows on which* KUANG-HSU *is lying. He looks up from his opium to pathetically ask:*)

KUANG-HSU: How can you love me? . . . How can you love me? . . .

(PEARL *stands looking out over the water, her hand gently touching the curve of her abdomen.*)

(*Lights change.*)

(*THE HALL OF SUPREME HARMONY.* TZU-HSI *is looking at the silver plate on which is the negative of* KUANG-HSU'S *image.*)

TZU-HSI: Once immortality was carved in marble. Now it's in shadow images made from a silver plate. (*She looks at it, then draws her long nails across the surface, ruining it.*) I think, if there are going to be immortal images, they had better be of me.

(LI *enters with the camera, borne by Servants. While she primps before a hand mirror, he prepares to take her photograph.*)

LI: You seem extremely happy today.

TZU-HSI: Having events in my own hands does wonders for my complexion.

LI: You look sixteen. How did you achieve this sudden onslaught of youth?

TZU-HSI: With great simplicity I have solved a problem which has been plaguing us for generations.

LI: Tell me—!

TZU-HSI: I have issued an ultimatum ordering the foreign delegations to leave Peking.

LI: A master stroke!

TZU-HSI: Within twenty-four hours.

LI: Empress, you are a genius! You look twelve! You look newborn!

TZU-HSI: Record it immediately!

(LI *takes her photograph. She primps for a different pose.* JUNG LU *enters.*)

JUNG LU: Is it true you've given the foreign delegations one day to leave Peking?

TZU-HSI: (*Posing*) It is true.

JUNG LU: How could you have done this?

TZU-HSI: I allowed them fifteen guards per legation. They asked permission to double that—and double that—and double that! Now there are more than two thousand "guards" making their way toward the capital. It's an invasion!

JUNG LU: You said you would not protect them against the attacks of the Boxers . . .

TZU-HSI: I said they should protect themselves. That does not mean summoning armies to Peking! (*Against her will, she has lost her temper. She checks her face in the mirror and pouts.*) You've made me look—twenty-nine! (*To* LI:) We will resume tomorrow. This is not how I choose to be immortalized.

(LI *exits with the camera.*)

JUNG LU: The legations are sending an envoy to talk to you.

TZU-HSI: They always want to talk, these Westerners!

JUNG LU: Will you see him?

TZU-HSI: Of course not. I've promised them safe conduct to their ships—

JUNG LU: Perhaps they want to ask for more time.

TZU-HSI: Time enough for their troops to get here? No! I want them out immediately!

JUNG LU: There is a rumor that they plan to ask for your resignation.

(*She laughs.*)

TZU-HSI: Ask? Ask *whom*? Who do they think they are, these brazen intruders, to think they have the right to interfere in our affairs!

(LI *enters, highly agitated.*)

What is it, Li?

Li: Empress—on his way here to the Forbidden City, the envoy from the foreign legations—has been killed.

Tzu-hsi: I *said* they should not count on conversations!

Jung Lu: What happened?

Li: He and his entourage were set upon in the street—

Jung Lu: By the Boxers?

Li: More than likely.

Tzu-hsi: It's the foreigners' own fault! Now they'll come to their senses and leave Peking immediately.

Li: On the contrary, they seem to be gathering in supplies for a long stay. Apparently they fear that you cannot—or will not—honor your promise of safe conduct.

Tzu-hsi: They dare doubt my word?

Li: The envoy and his entourage are dead. Even now the members of all the legations are gathering for safety in the British compound. There must be five hundred—almost half of them women and children.

Tzu-hsi: And just what do they intend to do there?

Li: Await the arrival of their relief force.

Tzu-hsi: And what do they expect *me* to do? Sit still while they march their combined forces to Peking? . . . I have no alternative but to declare war against the legations.

Jung Lu: You cannot declare war against the official representatives of Great Britain, France, Germany, Italy, Austria, Belgium, Holland, Japan, and the United States!

Tzu-hsi: I shall crush them in one blow. Quickly. And drive them into the sea.

Jung Lu: And have upon your head the vengeance of all the great powers?

Tzu-hsi: In this quarter of the earth, *China* is the only great power!

JUNG LU: These people have diplomatic immunity. It is against all civilized custom—

TZU-HSI: It is against all civilized custom for guests to treat their hosts with the condescension and contempt they have been heaping on us for centuries.

JUNG LU: I cannot be responsible if you declare an all-out war. How could I lead my army on a mission whose consequences would be so disastrous?

TZU-HSI: If your professional Army can't accomplish the task, the Boxers will drive them out.

JUNG LU: That pack of wild dogs? Who knows if they are loyal to the throne?

TZU-HSI: They, at least, have the courage to defend me.

JUNG LU: Your regular army has the courage to defend you!

TZU-HSI: Then this is your chance. Get the task done!

(JUNG LU *extis*. LI *approaches her*.)

LI: Empress, may I venture an opinion? . . . The Boxers are more fanatic about rooting out the foreigners than the regular army ever will be.

TZU-HSI: I know. But can the throne ally itself with beggars, thieves, and cutthroats?

LI: Beggars who can live through bullets. Cutthroats with supernatural powers.

(TZU-HSI *says nothing*.)

There is an old saying: If you have two hands, why use only one? . . . The Boxers only await your word to put all their passion—all their hatred—behind the fight for China.

TZU-HSI: (*After a pause*) . . . I will take advantage of this magic force—but no one must know. . . . Send Shen Tai to me.

(LI *exits*.)

So small an unprotected band of limp, pale Christians. Russian Christians who took from us—Central Asia. British Christians who took from us—Hong Kong! Burma! French Christians who took from us—Indo-China. And Japanese Buddhists who took from us—Korea. . . . They have all been a growing cancer for three centuries in China. But days from now—we will be cured!

(SHEN TAI *appears.* TZU-HSI *turns to him. Slowly she draws from her sleeve a thin band of bright red cloth.*)

TZU-HSI: Do you know what this is?

SHEN TAI: The headband of the Boxers.

(*She comes to him and ties it around his head.*)

TZU-HSI: You have played the hero, now you must *be* one.

SHEN TAI: I am not a soldier—

TZU-HSI: You are anything I say! You have the power to arouse multitudes. You have the power to harness this wild force and secretly make it serve my will.

SHEN TAI: What do you want me to do?

TZU-HSI: Arouse them! Direct them! Arm them!

SHEN TAI: I have no weapons—

(*She takes an emerald ring from her finger and gives it to him.*)

TZU-HSI: This will buy, I think, quite a few.

SHEN TAI: An emerald! Such beauty—!

TZU-HSI: It isn't beauty I give you, Shen Tai, it is power.

SHEN TAI: Power—

TZU-HSI: Isn't that what you have wanted all along?

(*He looks at her, then recognizes it.*)

SHEN TAI: Yes.

Tzu-hsi: "You have played the hero, now you must be one." (Shen Tai: Jonathan Fuller; Tzu-hsi: Ching Valdes, from the Cincinnati production. Photo copyright 1984 by Sandy Underwood.)

TZU-HSI: When you were powerless in the country, wasn't this what you dreamed of?

SHEN TAI: Yes, Empress!

TZU-HSI: Now I give you the power to liberate us all!

SHEN TAI: (*Aroused*) I can! I will! (*Slowly he begins to turn about, doing Kung-fu-like movements, hypnotizing himself into the trance of the Boxers. As he moves, he mutters magic incantations.*) Spirit of revenge, possess me! Spirit of the invincible, enter me and be my flesh! (*He whirls more and more swiftly until his arms grow strong, his legs sturdy, and his eyes burn with the fire of one possessed.*) Long live the Empress! (*Now the Boxer, he rushes out.*)

TZU-HSI: How miraculous it is that, just when I need them, this new force has arisen to deliver me. . . . We are a strange alliance, the Boxers and I, but together—we will win . . .

(*Lights change.*)

(*RAMPARTS OF THE FORBIDDEN CITY.* SHEN TAI, *standing on the ramparts, is illuminated in surrounding blackness. His head is thrown back, his red headband gleams. He cries out, exhorting unseen Boxer troops:*)

SHEN TAI: Fellow Boxers! Hear me! We are the avenging spirits! We are stronger than stone! Stronger than steel! I come to arouse you against the white plague which is upon us! Everywhere we are threatened by the round-eyed devils who have come from the west.

They outrage the spirit of our land. Their iron carriages disturb the terrestrial dragon and the land will not yield fruit to us! They have blackened the skies with their smoke and the heavens have gone dry! Their church spires pierce the realm of our gods, defiling their dwelling place! Everywhere their presence is a curse upon the landscape, and our gods are angry. They command us—get the blue-eyed devils out!

Only their blood can purify the streets of China! We Boxers are the force which shall make our nation clean! Bullets cannot harm us! We are indestructible!

Down with the foreign devils! Long live the Empress Tzu-hsi!

(*He runs out.*)

(*Lights change: THE IMPERIAL VIEWING PLATFORM. A hot midsummer day. Sounds of battle are heard in the distance.*)

(TZU-HSI *stands enthusiastically viewing the action through a spy-glass as a Servant shields her from the sun with an umbrella. The* WIFE *stands, fanning herself in the heat.*)

TZU-HSI: I love the beginning days of a battle! When the weak still think they can win! Come look at our men!

WIFE: I cannot look—

TZU-HSI: When I was a girl, I used to dress myself in armor and pretend to lead regiments into battle. If I were a girl now, I'd be on the wall with my men.

WIFE: May I be excused?

TZU-HSI: You may not! If there is this much going on before your eyes, you will view it! . . . How considerate of the foreigners to barricade themselves in the legation just beneath the Imperial Viewing Platform!

WIFE: It's so hot—

TZU-HSI: Good! The legations will be thirsty. They have only one small well.

(*We hear the buzz of a mosquito. The* WIFE *swats at it.*)

WIFE: I can't stand the mosquitoes!

TZU-HSI: You! Mosquitoes! Precious comrades! That way! Feast on the legations! . . . Look at them! With their pitiful supplies of food and ammunition. Look at their sandbags —made by the women out of their husbands' silk pajamas! . . . Let us make a wager of how long it will take us to completely crush them! Two days? Three? . . . Ask your husband if he would like to come witness this most glorious moment in all of China's history.

WIFE: He is ill, Empress.

TZU-HSI: Is he? I have never been so well!

(*A WOMAN'S VOICE is heard outside.*)

PEARL'S VOICE: I *will* see her!

(*As two guards try to stop her, the* PEARL *rushes in.*)

TZU-HSI: What is this impudence!

PEARL: I bring a message from the Kuang-hsu Emperor.

(TZU-HSI *dismisses the guards and Servant.*)

TZU-HSI: Is he dying?

PEARL: More slowly than you would like.

TZU-HSI: How did you get off the Ocean Terrace? Charmed the guards?

PEARL: The Kuang-hsu Emperor begs you to raise the seige of the legations.

TZU-HSI: Does he?

PEARL: He begs that you escort them safely to the coast—

TZU-HSI: Is he their ally?

PEARL: He thinks they should be treated with mercy.

TZU-HSI: His mind is befogged by the sweet haze *they* brought into China!

PEARL: It is *you* who have brought him to this! It is you who have forced him into a dream life, without living! Isolated! A prisoner! Spare him these indignities!

TZU-HSI: He is a weakling!

PEARL: He is the lawful ruler—!

TZU-HSI: Ah! You are brave! Brave as I was, you beauty! In spite of the fact that we both had nothing here! (*She touches* PEARL *roughly in the groin.*) Then it's so. You *are* pregnant! My eyes do not deceive me.

WIFE: She doesn't look pregnant—

TZU-HSI: It is a gift old women have—to divine the lump in the belly before it shows. (*She turns to* PEARL.) Whose child is this?

PEARL: The Emperor's.

TZU-HSI: He is as capable of impregnating you as I am! To whom have you opened your treasure?

PEARL: The Emperor.

WIFE: She must have used some kind of magic—

TZU-HSI: There will come a day when all men will be impotent. And we women will procreate ourselves—and rule forevermore . . . (*She puts her arm around* PEARL.) You needn't tell me who he was. I admire your descent into the darkness. You did as I did once. We could be sisters. Brave and young and beautiful. Can you believe that I was once brave and young and beautiful? . . . I still have the breasts of a woman young and strong. I need someone to be the self I was, someone who's more myself than I am. (*She touches* PEARL's *hair.*) You'll come live with me. You'll be my mirror. I'll look at myself—and I'll see you. You'll share my bed, and when I wake at night, instead of seeing the dark, I'll see youth and hope and beauty and salvation . . .

PEARL: I would rather share my bed with a thousand serpents!

TZU-HSI: Then go. But remember—I offered you life . . .

(PEARL *starts to exit the way she came.*)

Not that way.

(PEARL *stops.*)

Surely you don't think I'll allow you to return to Kuang-hsu. You are a clear mind. Too much of a luxury in prison. No. Let him dream about you—in your new home—the Garden of Dispossessed Favorites.

(PEARL's *face reveals what this separation will cost her, but she doesn't utter a sound.*)

You say nothing. . . . You do not beg. . . . If you weep before me, I will send you back to him.

PEARL: I shall never weep before you.

TZU-HSI: Go!

(PEARL *exits.*)

She is my young life . . .

(*The* WIFE *comes over to comfort her.* TZU-HSI *turns on her.*)

TZU-HSI: Leave me at once! Your face disgusts me!

(*The* Wife *exits.* Tzu-hsi *turns toward the battle.*)

Why does it take so long? It must go faster! Faster! (*We hear the sound of a mosquito. She smacks it dead on her hand. She rubs the bite.*) . . . Did we begin the battle on an auspicious day? I forgot to consult the mystic signs . . .

(*Lights change.*)

(*THE OCEAN TERRACE.* Kuang-Hsu, *now obviously in failing health, sits cross-legged on the floor surrounded by the dismembered pieces of the clock given to him by the British legation.*)

Kuang-Hsu: Time . . . In pieces . . . Broken . . . Not moving . . . Still, I notice, with time in pieces, the sun still rises, the sun still sets.

(*He shakes a mechanical bird, which has come off the clock.*)

Why don't you sing? Why won't you fly! Speak! Carry messages to her. Bring messages from her! Have you seen her in her garden? Tell me! (*He shakes the bird and breaks it. He screams at the clock face.*) Do not look upon me! Do not speak to me! I do not exist!

(*Despondently, he sits on the floor amidst the broken pieces. His* Wife *enters.*)

Wife: You shouldn't have taken it apart if you couldn't put it back together.

(Kuang-Hsu *turns away, still not acknowledging her existence.*)

Wife: Of all days, today you should be permitted to observe the battle.

(*He concentrates on the pieces of his clock, pretending not to hear.*)

Your aunt has ordered our soldiers to set fire to the great library next to the British legation. All of the new books you ordered. All of the old. The wind will fan the flames, destroy the legation, and the seige will come to an end!

(*He stops playing with the clock.*)

Wife: "You shouldn't have taken it apart if you couldn't put it back together." (Kuang-Hsu: Lester J.N. Mau; Wife: Carol A. Honda, from the Pan Asian production. Photo copyright 1984 by Corky Lee.)

You hear me! I know you hear me!

(*He is motionless.*)

Look at the smoke!

(*He looks up. He rises. He looks across the water, stunned and shaken. We can see the reflection of the flames.*)

KUANG-HSU: Our people set fire to our great library? All the future! All the past! In flames! All the ages! Burning, burning, burning, burning, burning! It is madness! (*He breaks down and sobs helplessly.*)

WIFE: The one who is mad—is you.

(*Lights change.*)

(*THE HALL OF SUPREME HARMONY. Night. Sporadic sounds of gunfire are heard in the distance.* Tzu-hsi *paces impatiently.*)

Tzu-hsi: Who changed the direction of the wind? The flames were supposed to consume the compound. The compound wasn't touched!

(Li *enters.*)

Li: This is certainly an inauspicious day—

Tzu-hsi: Why don't the legations fall? We have been battering at them for five weeks now! They have no food, no water. They have eaten their cow, their dogs, perhaps their own dead. Still they go on!

Li: Five weeks—

Tzu-hsi: I do, I believe, still comprehend the principles of simple logic. And this is what I wish to ask: Why, since they have only one cannon, since we are fighting on our own ground, since they are surrounded, since we have the higher position, more ammunition, more food, more men —*why can we not win?!!!*

(Li *takes a jewelled knife out of a sheath at his waist.*)

Li: Do you recognize this knife?

Tzu-hsi: It is the knife I gave Jung Lu—

Li: You know it has the power to sing of the brave deeds of its owner—

Tzu-hsi: It hasn't been with its owner for some time.

Li: Still, it will sing of his deeds. That is why I asked to keep it.

(Li *holds up the knife. He holds it up for some moments.*)

Tzu-hsi: I hear nothing.

(Li *holds up the knife again. Again there is nothing but silence.*)

Perhaps it sings too softly—

LI: Perhaps it does not sing at all.

TZU-HSI: What do you mean?

LI: Can it sing of a commander who stops his siege each day at sundown? Can it sing of a commander who orders his soldiers to shoot over his enemy's heads? Can it sing of a commander who sends his starving enemy wagonloads of fruit?

(*As* LI *speaks,* JUNG LU *slowly enters, his uniform grimy with the dust of battle.*)

TZU-HSI: Is this true?

JUNG LU: I am a soldier, not a butcher. I cannot command my men to fire on helpless women and children—

TZU-HSI: Helpless! They seem to be winning!

JUNG LU: There are laws of humanity—

TZU-HSI: Will you lose the war out of pity?

JUNG LU: You hold pity in such contempt! Our men marched to war with birdcages hung over their bayonets! They are tired of fighting!

TZU-HSI: So you fight a half-way war? Restoring in the evening the gains you made the day before? You are a traitor! . . . But what should I expect from a man who was lover to an Empress and chose to go to another's bed?

JUNG LU: Her bed was warm.

TZU-HSI: And mine?

JUNG LU: —is ice. And cruelty. Your greatest pleasure is destruction.

TZU-HSI: Your dying inside of me. Yes, I took pleasure in that.

JUNG LU: And now—in the deaths of thousands?

TZU-HSI: They are dying for a purpose—

JUNG LU: Is that how you justify giving your support secretly to the Boxers?

TZU-HSI: I am not answerable to you—

JUNG LU: *We cannot win!* I told you this before. You can slaughter the legations. Easily. But if you win against the legations, *still* you lose. The wrath of nine global powers will be upon you. You will be subject to retaliation of such force and from so many directions, that China as we know it will come to an end.

TZU-HSI: Then let it end! But let it end quickly! Let us not be eaten by them river by river, mind by mind! (*Suddenly her tone changes.*) Leave me! I do not wish to see anyone unless they bring me good news!

(LI *and* JUNG LU *exit.*)

(*Once* TZU-HSI *is alone, the weariness she has been trying to hide descends upon her. She sits on the throne.*)

Can it be that the force of the West is on the ascendancy? Can this hemisphere be moving into darkness? Will the light we held for centuries now illumine the other half of the globe while the dragon goes into eclipse? (*She falls to her knees.*) Great Buddha, what have we done to deserve your anger? Tell me what to do! Smile upon us! *Help* us!

(SHEN TAI *runs in, wildly elated, his clothes torn and bloody, his headband proudly askew on his head, his arms laden with plunder.*)

SHEN TAI: The city is a field of glory!

TZU-HSI: Tell me—!

SHEN TAI: Everything the foreigners have touched will be devoured in flames!

TZU-HSI: At last!

SHEN TAI: The streets are running with blood!

TZU-HSI: (*More to herself than to him.*) I have returned to the glorious days of my Manchu ancestors.

SHEN TAI: It's not that hard—real killing.

TZU-HSI: (*To herself*) They had the courage to ally themselves with darkness.

SHEN TAI: I thought of you—of serving you—

TZU-HSI: And you nobly performed your part. You are my hero, Shen Tai. My true hero. One day I will give you your own theatre. In it, you will show the victory of the dragon over the blue-eyed devils!

(JUNG LU *enters, looking more harassed and smoke-blackened than before.*)

JUNG LU: Your Boxers are beyond control! They've set the city aflame! They are attacking not only foreigners—but anyone at all!

TZU-HSI: My Boxers—

JUNG LU: I've sent for a relief force, but it hasn't arrived. You'll be lucky if there *is* a Peking by morning!

TZU-HSI: This is my ecstasy!

JUNG LU: It is not the foreign devils who are dying, it is your own people!

TZU-HSI: Only he who will go to the ends of his being can have a victory. I will dare everything! Burn everything! Even myself! I bless the holocaust—out of which will come a new beginning! (*She turns to* SHEN TAI.) Kill all foreigners. *Kill all foreigners.* I do not want *one* left alive in this land!

(SHEN TAI *bows obediently and runs out.*)

JUNG LU: I no longer recognize you—

TZU-HSI: If the heavens are harsh, I will be harsher. I won't go down without using every weapon that I have.

(JUNG LU *looks at her.* TZU-HSI *continues, deeply:*)

You have no idea what it is like to be up here. You think, once you are in power, you can bend events to your will. The splendid joke is—in the seat of power, you are more powerless than ever! It's in the fates, or in the hands of heaven. And there's nothing, nothing you can do! I can endure anything, but I can't endure being helpless!

(*She buries her face in her hands.* JUNG LU *comes to her and gently takes her hands away from her face.*)

Can you bear to touch an old lady?

JUNG LU: I can bear it.

TZU-HSI: You are the only one on Earth to whom I've ever shown my private face.

JUNG LU: I know. You exist by wearing the mask of cruelty. It's your survival.

TZU-HSI: How did you manage to survive when I stripped you of everything? Why did you not break?

JUNG LU: I bent to the will of heaven, and so rode out the storm.

TZU-HSI: Bending is an undignified posture.

JUNG LU: Sometimes it's the most powerful one there is.

TZU-HSI: (*Suddenly cold*) You're trying to give me hints—

JUNG LU: You never could stand being told anything.

TZU-HSI: It was such a relief when you were banished. There was no one around to think they could tell me what to do.

JUNG LU: Your loss.

TZU-HSI: Brazen bull!

JUNG LU: Stubborn bitch!

TZU-HSI: I could have you executed for that!

JUNG LU: Fine! Then I won't have to watch you lead the country to ruin!

TZU-HSI: (*Icily*) And just what course do you think I should pursue?

JUNG LU: I think you should *talk*! I think you should be in communication with your enemies. I think you should tear down the walls surrounding the Forbidden City and become a part of *life*!

(TZU-HSI *turns away*.)

Eye-to-eye is the only way this country will be saved. You think they're barbarians. They think *we're* barbarians. We will never understand each other until we can see ourselves through each other's eyes. Meet, in the same room, face to face.

TZU-HSI: I can't seem weak, I can't seem womanly—

JUNG LU: All I'm asking you to do is seem *human*. . . . The last time I felt you were human was the night you and I said farewell. You left the next morning to become the Emperor's concubine. Since then—

TZU-HSI: (*Extremely vulnerable*) Since then—I have lived in the fear that all this would be taken from me. There is no moment when I actually believe I have it.

JUNG LU: It cannot be taken from you by people who respect and understand you. . . . See the representatives of the legations.

(TZU-HSI *looks at him*.)

It is the only way that will not lead to total mutual disaster.

(TZU-HSI *considers this a long time, then at last says*:)

TZU-HSI: Very well. Tell them I will receive them.

JUNG LU: I doubt very much that they would enter the Forbidden City. They would suspect an ambush. *You* must go to *them*.

TZU-HSI: Me to them! Like a simpering beggar—!

JUNG LU: Like a great woman. The illustrious, all-forgiving, beneficent ruler of five hundred million.

TZU-HSI: (*Simply*) Do you think—outside these walls — without the mystery and grandeur of the throne room— that I can impress those white men?

Jung Lu: I think you can dazzle them.

Tzu-hsi: It would surprise them, wouldn't it? An imperial procession—straight through the legations' streets!

Jung Lu: They would be astounded. Six armies couldn't accomplish what could be accomplished by one woman using her mind.

Tzu-hsi: (*After considering*) ... Then I'll do it! Single-handedly, I'll end the war! I've always wanted to be a soldier!

Jung Lu: A soldier of reason.

(Li *enters.*)

Tzu-hsi: Prepare my travelling chair, Li. I am going on a small journey.

Li: Empress—

Tzu-hsi: Bring me my jewels, bring me my imperial robe—

Li: Empress, the relief force has arrived.

Tzu-hsi: At last!

Li: *Their* relief force. Not ours.

(*We hear the fife and drum of the Allied armies.*)

Thirty-thousand men. Twice as many as we can muster.

Jung Lu: Then it's over.

Tzu-hsi: No! I am going out to talk with them!

Jung Lu: It just became too late for reason.

Tzu-hsi: We must try—

Jung Lu: Too late. . . . Too late. . . .

(*Lights change.*)

(*THE GATE OF SPIRITUAL VALOR. Sounds of invading soldiers, shouting in various languages, are heard in the distance. The Drum of Remonstrance sits silently in the foreground. The* Wife *runs in, followed by* Kuang-Hsu.)

WIFE: The guards have fled! There's no one here! No one to protect us!

(JUNG LU *enters.*)

JUNG LU: I'll protect you.

KUANG-HSU: (*Very formally dressed and coiffed. He speaks in the low Emperor's voice that* SHEN TAI *taught him.*) This is a very fine robe. We must thank our tailor.

JUNG LU: Emperor, I am taking you to the camp of the foreigners. You must not be afraid.

KUANG-HSU: (*He takes out a string of paper soldiers.*) I have the loyal support of my soldiers. I have only to breathe on them to make them come alive.

JUNG LU: You must be the figurehead around which China can rally. The foreigners are not against all of us. They are against *her*. They will restore you to the throne. They will support you.

KUANG-HSU: (*Holding up the soldiers*) Shall I breathe on them now?

(*Seeing the Emperor's madness,* JUNG LU *makes a gesture of despair.*)

(*The* PEARL CONCUBINE *suddenly appears. Her robes are bedraggled. Her pregnancy is beginning to show. She stares at the Emperor, whom she has not seen in many weeks.*)

KUANG-HSU: I was not aware that I was to choose new concubines this morning. Who is this one?

PEARL: (*Sensing his madness and coming toward him with compassion.*) My love—

KUANG-HSU: Do not speak to me! Do not hear! Do not look upon the Emperor!

(*She moves away, deeply moved and holding back her sorrow.* KUANG-HSU *observes her coolly.*)

She is too fat, that one. Her belly is too round. Rejected! Rejected!

(Li *enters, pulling a cart on which are piled old clothes.*)

Li: The foreign soldiers are at the southern gate to the Forbidden City. We must disguise ourselves as peasants. We must escape to the north—to the Summer Palace. I have hidden the Great Seal and the imperial jewels. We must hurry—

(*He starts handing out the clothing.* Tzu-hsi *enters.*)

You must disguise yourself as a peasant.

(*He tries to give her old clothes.*)

Tzu-hsi: A peasant!—Never! (*She thrusts the clothes away.*) I will not be cheated out of my encounter. If I cannot go to them, I shall address them from the wall. (*She mounts the highest place on the ramparts and cries out:*) Diplomats and soldiers of the allied nations! Listen to me! I am the Dowager Empress! I am the one whose face you've never seen!

In one moment, you will have breached our walls. . . . It is too late for talk. But it is not too late for steel. Who will take his sword in hand and meet me blade to blade in single combat? Let this battle be decided one to one! . . . Come! Anyone!

Jung Lu: You are mad!

Tzu-hsi: Stay away!

(*He obeys. She stands alone.*)

What? No one? . . . Then aim your rifles! Aim them to this heart and slay the dragon—! (*She stands with arms outstretched, facing us, a willing target. But no shots ring out.*)

Jung Lu: Come down from there—!

Tzu-hsi: (*Disappointed*) They will not shoot. (*Reluctantly, she turns and descends.*) They hold me in such contempt that I am not worth killing.

Jung Lu: They would not martyr you. It would arouse the sympathy of the world.

Tzu-hsi: Well, what they cannot achieve for me, I can achieve myself . . .

Tzu-hsi: "What they cannot achieve for me, I can achieve myself. . . ." (Tzu-hsi: Tina Chen, from the Pan Asian production. Photo copyright 1984 by Corky Lee.)

(She holds a small vial in her hand. She opens the vial and starts to raise it to her lips—but hesitates.)

(As she stands frozen, undecided, the PEARL *says, deeply:)*

PEARL: Do not hesitate. Let the country go. You have possessed the land for nearly half a century. It is you who have held her to the past and brought her to this. Release it from your ancient hands, I beg you. Dispatch yourself —and let China live!

TZU-HSI: (*Quietly, after a moment*) . . . How lovely it is that the most charming, the most beautiful, the most merciful among you most ardently desires my death. (*She looks slowly, from one to another.*) That would be a great solution, wouldn't it? A solution for you. A solution for me. . . . And how will China live? Under Kuang-hsu the weak? (*She looks at* JUNG LU.) So you are going to take him to the foreigners and have them seat him as their puppet on his own throne? . . . No! No! I may be ancient, but I will resist with every fibre of my being this humiliating mockery of China's former glory. (*She turns to the* Pearl, *lovingly.*) I thank you, my brave one, my Pearl, for bringing me to life again. You alone—see with the eyes of my youth. You see how much I hoped for—and how much I failed. . . . I can't bear what you see. . . . For knowing me too well, seeing me too clearly, you must die, Pearl. (*She has spoken this sadly.*)

Jung Lu: (*To the* Pearl) Run! There's no one here to carry out her order—

(Pearl *turns to* Kuang-Hsu.)

Pearl: My love—

Kuang-Hsu: Rejected . . .

(*The* Pearl Concubine *bows to* Kuang-Hsu *who, busy with his paper soldiers, hardly even notices her. Slowly, with dignity, the* Pearl *walks out.* Tzu-hsi *calls:*)

Tzu-hsi: If there is anyone within the sound of my voice who is still loyal to me, dispatch this traitor! (*She turns to* Li.) Li, bring me my royal gown.

(*She stands as he puts over her imperial robe a ragged peasant coat.*)

Now, cut my nails, they only took a lifetime to grow.

(*He removes her nail protectors, kneeling at her feet.*)

Now, remove my headdress . . .

(*He performs this task—the ceremonial divesting of the last shred of royalty.*)

I see a glorious future for China.

Jung Lu: (*Bitterly*) A future under you . . .

Tzu-hsi: It is heaven's will. . . . If the Dynasty were to end, the Drum of Remonstrance would be sounded. But see? it is absolutely silent. I still possess the Mandate of Heaven.

(SHEN TAI *enters, looking stunned.*)

SHEN TAI: The Pearl is at the bottom of the well. I drowned her. I heard you call out to kill and I obeyed. Even when I saw it was the Pearl, I kept on killing. Obeying you . . .

I shoved her into the well. She resisted at first, but then it seemed she fell into her reflection gladly. . . . But what was it? As she disappeared beneath the water, somewhere I thought I heard the crying of a child.

TZU-HSI: Did you not know she was carrying your child?

SHEN TAI: My child! I have killed my child! What have you made me do? What have you made us *all* do? *Monster!*

(*He lurches toward* TZU-HSI *threateningly, but cannot bring himself to touch her. He cries out in anger and collapses on the ground.*)

TZU-HSI: So you, too, desire my death. . . . Why don't you kill me, all of you? You are many, I am one. (*She looks each one in the eye. No one moves. She says, deeply, wearily:*) I am, still am, the only one who can hold this country together.

(*The walls are breached. The shouts, the gunfire, and the fife and drum of the attacking soldiers are heard, much nearer.*)

(TZU-HSI *gestures toward* LI *and* JUNG LU.)

TZU-HSI: You. Oxen. Hitch yourselves to my cart.

(*On his way to the cart,* KUANG-HSU *passes* TZU-HSI. *Holding his paper soldiers, he asks her:*)

KUANG-HSU: Shall I breathe on them now?

(TZU-HSI *touches his face in pity. She,* KUANG-HSU, *and the* WIFE *get into the cart. The cart begins to move. As it passes* SHEN TAI, *he cries out.*)

SHEN TAI: I once worshipped you! (*He breaks down, weeping.*)

Tzu-hsi: "So you, too, desire my death. . . . Why don't you kill me, all of you?" (Shen Tai: Mel Gionson; Jung Lu: Alvin Lum; Tzu-hsi: Tina Chen; Li: Tom Matsusaka; Wife: Carol A. Honda; Kuang-Hsu: Lester J.N. Mau, from the Pan Asian production. Photo copyright 1984 by Corky Lee.)

TZU-HSI: Dry your eyes! Rejoice! As long as I live, China is living! Why do you weep? *I survive!*

(JUNG LU *and* LI *pull out the cart with* TZU-HSI, KUANG-HSU, *and the* WIFE *on it.* SHEN TAI *rises, pulling off his red headband. He cries out:*)

SHEN TAI: I, too, survive!

(*He runs over to the Drum of Remonstrance. He starts to pound upon it with his fists. With all the power in his soul, he beats upon the drum in rage and rebellion.*)

(JUNG LU *appears in a light at another part of the stage. As the rhythmic pounding continues in pantomime,* JUNG LU *says:*)

JUNG LU: As the Empress Tzu-hsi retreated to her summer palace, she saw China for the first time—her subjects and their poverty, as the Tutor and I had described them. But

Tzu-hsi: "As long as I live, China is living! Why do you weep? I survive!" Shen Tai: "I, too, survive!" (At the Drum of Remonstrance: Shen Tai: Jonathan Fuller; On the cart: Tzu-hsi: Ching Valdes, and members of the Court, from the Cincinnati production. Photo copyright 1984 by Sandy Underwood.)

the foreign powers, their victory complete, found themselves compelled to look to Tzu-hsi as the only leader who commanded enough obedience and respect to be restored to the Dragon Throne.

Less than a year after her flight, the Empress was welcomed back to Peking in a magnificent triumphal procession. She ruled for eight more years, gradually instituting many of the reforms Kuang-hsu and the Tutor had advocated—even proposing a constitutional monarchy.

But it was all too late. In a bankrupt China, Tzu-hsi, still ruler of the Empire, died a peaceful death on November 15, 1908 at the age of seventy-three. Her nephew, the Emperor Kuang-hsu, had died the very day before.

The Empress's appointed heir to the throne was my two-year-old grandson, Prince P'u-i. He sustained the more than 4000-year-old Imperial Throne for three more years until he was deposed by the First Republic. P'u-i was the last Chinese Emperor. He died, a poor government clerk, in the People's Republic of China in 1967.

(*The lights fade on* JUNG LU.)

(SHEN TAI'S *pounding on the Drum increases in pace and loudness. Now wearing a Mao cap, he pounds his fists on the Drum, loudly signalling the end of the Dynasty's Mandate from Heaven.*)

(*The pounding of the Drum grows to a tremendous climax.*)

BLACKOUT

END ACT TWO

PRODUCTION NOTES

Empress of China may be presented at any one of several levels of production, from the most basic to the most elaborate.

BASIC
The Pan Asian Repertory Theatre production in New York, directed by Tisa Chang, used a simple platform similar to a Shakespearean thrust stage. Eight actors performed the play on an almost bare stage without the assistance of any nonspeaking servants or extras. On Bob Phillip's set, changes of place were indicated mainly by changes in lighting.

As written, every scene in the play has at least one physical element or prop—the axe, the clocks, the red headband, etc.—that is the visual and symbolic key to the scene. In this production, these were carried in and removed by the actors. A croquet mallet was substituted for the bicycle. Original background music was on tape.

MODERATE
A second, slightly more elaborate, level of production is reflected in the script herein. A certain amount of scenic elaboration is indicated. The suggestion is for a unit set, with the use of banners or screens to suggest changes of place. These changes may be effected mechanically or by the use of four or more Servants whose presence has been suggested within the scenes. Not only do these nonspeaking extras perform tasks that realistically would not be carried out by members of the Imperial Court; their presence adds atmosphere and suggests the ceremonial stratified life within the Forbidden City.

AUGMENTED
A third, still more elaborate, level of production was reflected by the Cincinnati Playhouse production, directed by Robert Kalfin. Here, Michael Sharp's set utilized a

turntable within a turntable. On the center turntable were two eight-foot square boxes, one on top of the other, which opened and closed to reveal scenes. On its reverse side, the turntable had three broad flights of steps leading up to the elevated Dragon Throne. Some locations moved in on the outer turntable. Projections on scrim were also used to indicate change of place.

This production added a chorus of eight who at various times played Concubines, Eunuchs, or Peasants. They not only moved scenery and attended at the court, but appeared in eight "Illusions"—musical and mime numbers that were interpolated into the show. These Illusions, conceived of by Kalfin and directed by him and choreographed by Dania Krupska, were: Shen Tai Performs the Story of Tzu-hsi's Life; Tzu-hsi Performs the Story of Her Life; The Boxer Threat; Shen Tai Performs the True Story of Tzu-hsi's Life; Sir Claude's Vaudeville; Shen Tai on the Ramparts; The Boxers Attack the Foreigners; and Shen Tai Pursues the Pearl Concubine.

In this production, three Musicians, seated on stage, played more than thirty instruments, from Chinese gong, cymbal, and flute to synthesizer. Their music accompanied much of the action.

The complexity of the production of *Empress of China* is at the discretion of the director. But, whatever the level of production, it is to be hoped that the physical elements will not overwhelm the inner life of the characters and play. Although the specific story is Chinese, the ideas, of revolution and reaction, of power and powerlessness, of love of the future vs. love of the past, are universal. Therefore, the slavish reconstruction of a specific time and place in scenery and costumes is to be avoided. The best production will be one that exercises the imagination, using elements of the past creatively to present a vision of a theme that is definitely of the *Now*.

RUTH WOLFF

MOLLY BAILEY'S TRAVELING FAMILY CIRCUS featuring SCENES FROM THE LIFE OF MOTHER JONES

BY MEGAN TERRY and JOANNE METCALF

A musical presentation of magical and possible events in the lives of **two women** born in the last century. The Omaha Magic Theater (where **Megan Terry** is the playwright in residence) has toured this show around the Mid West. A minimum of three males and four females, though it can be expanded to accommodate a greater number; may be done with simple fluid staging.

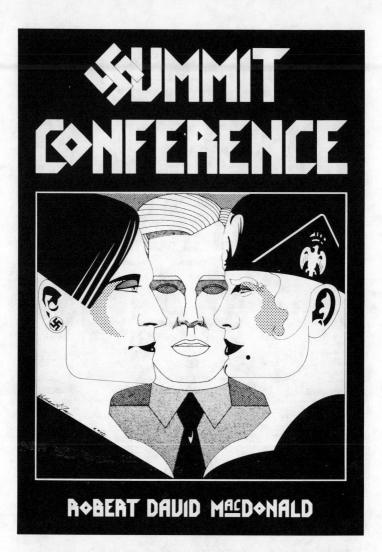

SUMMIT CONFERENCE

ROBERT DAVID MacDONALD

Set in the Berlin chancellery in 1941, this play is a fictional encounter between the mistresses of **Hitler and Mussolini:** Eva Braun and Clara Petacci. This show had a successful run in **London's West End** in 1982 with **Glenda Jackson.** There are some restrictions on production rights.

In this **one-man show** set in a Monte Carlo villa at the end of the last century, the grand master of the kitchen, Escoffier, ponders a glorious return from retirement. In doing so, he relates anecdotes about the famous and shares his mouth-watering recipes with the audience. One male; single interior set.

One Acts
~ And ~
Monologues
~ For ~

Women

BY~LUDMILLA BOLLOW

These haunting plays mark the arrival of a **new voice in the American Theater**. Two of the three pieces in this volume, THE WOMAN WITH 27 CHILDREN and BELLE OF THE BIJOU are monologues approximately thirty-five minutes in length. LATE/LATE . . . COMPUTER DATE is a forty minute one-act for two women. All three call for simple interior sets.

This delightful small scale **musical** is about the life of **Gilbert and Sullivan**. It is interspersed with some of the best known songs from the Savoy operas, including THE PIRATES OF PENZANCE, HMS PINAFORE and THE MIKADO. This show had a very successful run on the West End of London in 1975, and subsequently at the **Actors Theater of Louisville**. Five males, three females, though more actors may be used as "stage-hands" and chorus members.

NATIVE SPEECH

BY ERIC OVERMYER

A riveting play, rich in texture and rife with allusion, which provides a chilling vision of civilization about to go belly up. Originally produced at the **Los Angeles Theater Center** in the summer of 1983. Seven males, three females, though one more of each can be used. Single interior set plus an exterior playing area.

Poisonous mushrooms, red herrings, marital infidelities, and a mysterious Merchant of Death are elements in this English style **thriller** with a fascinating, intricate plot. Four males, two females; single interior set.

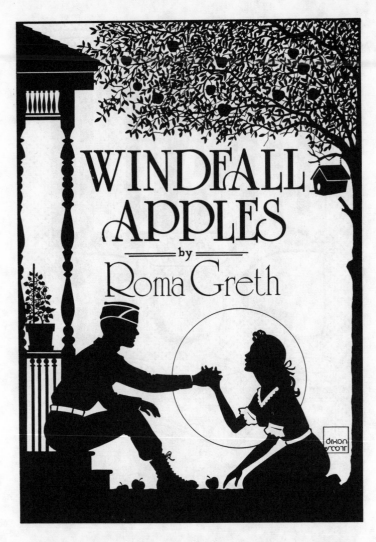

WINDFALL APPLES
by
Roma Greth

This gem of a play evokes the **days of youth and innocence** as our boys were being shipped off to World War II. This play workshopped at the **Eugene O'Neill Theater Center** in the summer of 1977, and then was produced in Manhattan at the IRT late in 1978. Three males, three females; single interior and exterior set.

LOOKING-GLASS

by Michael Sutton and Cynthia Mandelberg

This provocative chronicle, interspersed with fantasy sequences from
ALICE IN WONDERLAND, traces the career of Charles Dodgson (better known as **Lewis Carroll**) from his first work on the immortal classic,
to his near downfall when accused of immorality. First produced at the
Entermedia Theater on Second Ave in June of 1982. Six males, four
females with some doubling.

SAGA

by Kelly Hamilton

This wonderful **musical** is a history of America's pioneers as they push their way across the country. A minimum of eight males and eight females are necessary, and the show can be expanded to use many more actors. Settings can be fluid and simple or elaborate.